INDIANS MUST KNOW
LET'S BE PROUD

SHRINIVAS

INDIA · SINGAPORE · MALAYSIA

Notion Press

Old No. 38, New No. 6
McNichols Road, Chetpet
Chennai - 600 031

First Published by Notion Press 2019
Copyright © Shrinivas 2019
All Rights Reserved.

ISBN 978-1-64587-295-5

This book has been published with all efforts taken to make the material error-free after the consent of the author. However, the author and the publisher do not assume and hereby disclaim any liability to any party for any loss, damage, or disruption caused by errors or omissions, whether such errors or omissions result from negligence, accident, or any other cause.

While every effort has been made to avoid any mistake or omission, this publication is being sold on the condition and understanding that neither the author nor the publishers or printers would be liable in any manner to any person by reason of any mistake or omission in this publication or for any action taken or omitted to be taken or advice rendered or accepted on the basis of this work. For any defect in printing or binding the publishers will be liable only to replace the defective copy by another copy of this work then available.

Dedicated to

My Granny Mai
who inculcated nationalism in me.

यदा यदा हि धर्मस्य ग्लानिर्भव - ति भारत ।
अभ्युत्थान - मधर्मस्य तदात्मानं सृजाम्यहम् - ॥४-७॥
परित्राणाय - साधूनां विनाशाय च दुष्कृताम् - ।
धर्मसंस्था - पनार्थाय सम्भवामि युगे युगे ॥४-८॥

"Whenever there is decay of righteousness, O Bharata, And there is exaltation of unrighteousness, then I Myself come forth; For the protection of the good, for the destruction of evil-doers, For the sake of firmly establishing righteousness, I am born from age to age."

"Until the lion tells his side of the story, the tale of the hunt will always glorify the hunter."

– An African Proverb

Contents

Preface viii
Acknowledgement x

1. Alexander – Not so Great!................................1
2. The First Emperor of India 9
3. Battle of Delhi 19
4. Vishwavidyalaya 29
5. Mighty Vijaynagaram 38
6. Ahomic War 47
7. The User Manuals 56
8. Coast Guards 66
9. Kannadi Queens 75
10. India's Contribution to the World 86
11. Avatars of Shakti 94
12. Land of Saints 102
13. The Largest Surrender 111
14. Women Against British 120

Preface

British historians, and sadly, even Indian historians, airbrushed only the things that won't bring pride in our hearts about our country. Even the school books finish the glorious history in a mere few paragraphs. The generations are not engineered to love India but feel sorry about the country. Everyone in this country knows the names of Mughal emperors for the streets are named after them, but their contribution to humanity is of little use.

We Indians hardly know the names of the kings who changed this land into a gold mine. If we take the example of our most ancient civilisation, i.e., Harappa, we only know that they had a state-of-the-art sewage system, but they were much more than just waste managers. Some history was purposefully hidden by the pre – and post-independence governments. There are many stories in which only one side is presented to us. Furthermore, today's media deliberately keeps positive things away from the crowd and focuses on negative news. We term the Western things 'modern' and our own culture 'obsolete' where a spiritual person is considered uninteresting, and a movie featuring a drug addict can earn you 500 crores.

Preface

Our country should understand who our real heroes are and who the reel heroes are. If we don't respect our real heroes, our monuments, and our culture, no one else will respect them either. India, since the last few centuries, has been a victim of false narratives about our history. This led to a decrease in integrity in our country. The Western movies show that India is only about Taj Mahal and snake charmers. Our own cinema has contributed very less to enlighten us about our splendid past. Our high tolerance and inclusiveness were always taken as weakness by the world. Our educational system is highly responsible for the Westernised mentality. Education in India is only about marks and history is just another subject to score marks. No one is taught to learn something from history. We have termed *Ramayana* and *Mahabharata* the great epics of our culture as 'mythology' and not history. We have dealt ourselves in the debates about the occurrences of these epics but have not learnt anything from them. We found interest in *'Yog'* when it became 'Yoga'. Hence it is now the high time to feel proud of our magnificent culture and glorious past.

Acknowledgement

It is very difficult for an individual to create valuable materials by himself. But when that creation is taken care of by many hands, the tough task becomes a cakewalk. This debut book of mine, for my beautiful country, has many such hands that are worth acknowledging. To start with, I thank Lord Ram for blessing me with this great life and creating favourable situations around me to do something that I love doing. I thank Him for choosing *Bharat* as my birthplace. Being a devotee of Lord Ganesh succoured me in creating this piece of work. I would thank my parents who imbibed in me great human values and tremendous love for my country. My father, Surendra Hinge, encouraged me in writing some stories and also discussed some nuances of writing as he is a writer himself. My mother, Namrata Hinge, who is my critic, as well as a true fan of my writings, helped me in improving my work. The teachings of my grandpa, Jayant Keshav Vaze, made me a responsible citizen of this nation. This book is an outcome of his lessons.

My wife, Hemangi, who was my first reader, gave me the first-hand response about the stories. My sister, Prajakta, deserves a special mention for appreciating me and also criticising my work wherever necessary,

Acknowledgement

which helped me to write better. My aunt, Rupali, an avid reader who has a great understanding of writing, assisted me in this journey of book writing. Priya Keskar, my aunt, guided me in the usage of accurate language while writing. Chaitra, my niece, was a peephole for me into the younger generation's thinking and their likes. This book looks better because of the two artists I have in my life—my dear friends, Chirag Date and Atharva Kulkarni—who drew the sketches and made this book more attractive.

Many books I read helped me with the content I had to share in this book. Six glorious epochs of Indian history by V. D Savarkar (Avinash Inamdar, I thank you for gifting me this book at the right time), books like *The Land of Seven Rivers* and *The Incredible History of India's Geography* by Sanjeev Sanyal helped me a lot. Amish, the author of *Immortal India*, motivated me with his writings. *Indians Must Know* contains facts mentioned by Swami Vivekananda in his work. Last but not least, thanks to the internet for the ocean of knowledge I gathered from authentic websites.

A special thanks to Sadhguru Jaggi Vasudev for making me believe that I am capable of doing something that I could not have imagined a couple of years ago. I am so fortunate to take birth in the era where you coexist with me to constantly bless me, motivate me and also scold me whenever necessary. Last but not least, I extend gratitude to all the virtuous and magnificent people because of whom the righteousness persisted. I bow down to those who made my country the best place to live in.

Alexander – Not so Great!

He suddenly woke up from a deep sleep. He looked worried and frightened. Though the night was cold, perspiration ran down his forehead. Alexander looked at both sides; no one was there in the room. There was pin-drop silence. His chest was still hurting a lot because the worst incident ever happened to him in the most adventurous expedition carried out by his Macedonians. Alexander was wounded, physically and mentally. His biggest ambition in life, of conquering the world, was tarnished by now. The only ambition he had now was to survive in the desert. Such panic attacks were common those days. He tried his best to forget that part of the year 326 BC when his only dream in life got busted. His ten long years' endeavours went in vain. He tried every possible course of action to achieve his dream. There was so much manoeuvring going on within the family to enthrone himself after his father's death when he was 19 years old. He betrayed so many associates and cousins who trusted him so that he could occupy the throne. He forgave none of his enemies and killed each one to march towards his aim of conquering the world.

He was also famously known as the destroyer of faith. He had no respect for others' faith or belief systems. One day, when he was extremely inebriated, he ordered to burn all the available texts, the priests and the holy book, *Avesta* of the Zoroastrians (Parsees). This had a massive impact on the Zoroastrian community, and there was a decline in the Parsee faith. In today's world, Parsees are almost extinct; hence preserving the text and religious scriptures are very important to sustain the religion. Alexander also used the cruel policy of divide and rule wherever possible. But all these tactics worked only till 326 BC.

After destroying Persian kingdoms and crushing their sovereignty, Alexander's next target was the land of the seven rivers, i.e., Bharat. He had heard many astounding stories of this land. The Macedonian emperor was eager to see this land. He wanted to rule the land that was a superpower. This Greek emperor was waiting impatiently to be the emperor of the empire in which everyone was extremely rich and prosperous. Alexander, with his full might, started marching towards India. According to the Greeks, the Indian Ocean was the end of the world; anyone who conquered the provinces up until the Indian Ocean was deemed to have won the world. So he aimed to reach the Indian Ocean and become the emperor of the whole world. Every night he envisioned this dream. He was triumphant in all his wars till then and was expecting the same in the future, but fate had decided something else for Alexander.

He faced massive opposition as he entered Indian borders. As he entered present-day Afghanistan, the *Ashvayanas*, the local Afghan tribe, fought against him. They were the indigenous Afghans. They were the forefathers of the Afghan people and ruled in the areas of Kumar, Swat, Buner and Peshawar valleys, which are now a part of Pakistan and Afghanistan. Alexander managed to crush the revolt of the tribal people.

The areas full of mountains stopped the advance of Alexander. Alexander's major battles took place in the deserts, but now the terrain and climate were new and different for him and for his army. Massaga, Bazira and Ora were some of the places, which were very small kingdoms but fought bravely with Alexander. The first war took place with the Massaga kingdom. A ferocious battle was fought between the Macedonian army and Massaga. But unfortunately, the king of Massaga fell in the battle and lost his life. But the subjects of the king didn't stop fighting. This came up as a surprise for Alexander. Every battle he had fought till that day, if the king died, the subjects would surrender and accept Alexander's dominance. Such a response was not familiar to the Macedonian chief.

After the fall of the king, his mother took charge, gathered lion-hearted men and women of the land to fight against the Macedonians. Alexander was not ready for such a response. It vexed him. He had defeated huge forces, but now a small kingdom had disturbed all his planning. He had to retreat from the battle. Macedonians brainstormed to come up with another plan. Alexander understood that he could not win over Massaga in an ethical way. He began to play evil games. He went into a no-war pact with Massaga. The lady commander agreed with Alexander and trusted him; she was unable to read the backstabbing message between the lines. Massaga was delighted, and on the same night, they started the celebration of their strategic victory. The city went to sleep with a pleasant mood, and everyone was fully inebriated. Alexander ordered his troops to march towards Massaga when the whole city was in a deep sleep. They accepted his command and massacred the whole city. The same thing happened at Ora. Indians were not aware that anyone could go to such a cruel extent to win wars. Such an extreme level of betrayal was almost a foreign concept to Indians during those days.

Alexander's next stop was Takshashila. Takshashila is a province in today's Pakistan. Takshashila city was famous for having the largest educational hub. Alexander received information from his spies that there were two kings named Porus and Ambhi. Both were fierce enemies of each other. He sent troops to both kings asking them to either surrender or fight against the large Macedonian army. Ambhi, being aware of Alexander's power, surrendered immediately. But King Porus of Paurava rejected Alexander's truce. Instead, he started preparing for the war, which was very much inevitable considering Alexander's ambitions and reputation. Ambhi was sure that Paurava, though a prosperous kingdom, was weaker in front of the Macedonian empire. So, he joined Alexander against Porus on the terms that after defeating the Paurava Kingdom, Alexander would make him the king of both the kingdoms, Takshashila and Paurava. Alexander agreed to his terms.

Alexander – Not so Great!

The lore describes Porus as a very strong and magnificent man. He was seven feet tall, muscular and witty too. He was famous in the entire Bharat for his leadership qualities. Meanwhile, Chanakya, a learned scholar and a teacher at Takshashila University, started a movement in India where there was an upsurge of need in India to stop the invasion of any outside forces.

Alexander, with Ambhi, decided to attack Paurava. The main hurdle for the large Macedonian army was the river Jhelum. So they found a route where the river wouldn't trouble them. They found an area with small tributaries of Jhelum, which was not deep so that the army could easily locomote.

Porus came to know of the advance of Alexander's army, so he sent his son with a small battalion to understand the whereabouts of the invaders and stop them if possible. But to his surprise, the enemy had a full-fledged preparation. They were left with no option but to fight. There was a skirmish between both the armies. In that battle, Porus' son was killed. This enraged Porus tremendously. He decided to launch the final attack to destroy the Macedonians. His army consisted of 20,000 infantrymen, 2,000 cavalry and 200 war elephants. Paurava's army marched towards the Macedonians. Alexander, accompanied by Ambhi, had a combined army of 34,000 infantrymen and 7,000 cavalry. He was confident that they would outnumber Porus' army. They also contemplated Porus' tactics that he might use to fight the war, which can be a great advantage for the invader.

Both the armies stood facing each other waiting for the command from their masters. But then, Alexander saw something that he had never imagined. The land started shaking as if there was an earthquake. Everyone in the Greek army looked petrified. There was a loud noise approaching from the dense trees behind Porus' army, suggesting some humungous objects speeding towards the war zone. The Macedonians were clueless. All of a sudden, huge elephants in a large number appeared from behind the trees from the dense forest and trumpeted loudly in unison. It was a deafening noise. The elephants' size was much larger than what Alexander had expected. There was a provision on the elephant where not just the Mahout (elephant rider) but some more men could fight standing on the mammoth animal. They could shoot arrows in all directions while standing on it. It was a tremendous shock for the Greeks as they were completely unaware of Porus' preparations.

Commanders of both the armies gave orders to their respective men to attack each other with full force. The land vibrated as the elephants marched towards the Macedonians. The Macedonian horses went berserk after seeing the huge elephants running towards them. Many horses were killed by these elephants. Elephants tore apart Alexander's men with their trunks. This was not it. The skilled Paurava army had peculiar arrows and bows; the arrows were two metres long, which could pierce through more than one enemy at a time. Alexander's army had never faced such a situation in a decade.

Suddenly, there was heavy rainfall during the war, which confused both the armies. Macedonians had no experience of fighting in such weather conditions. Porus' army also faced some trouble due to rain. The elephants' legs jammed into the mud. The biggest assets of Porus' army were now turning against them. The elephants got extremely disturbed, creating chaos on the battlefield against the Paurvas' favour.

Porus fought bravely in this battle. He knew this battle was do or die for his kingdom. He put all his power into the battle. Alexander, on the other hand, was shattered. He had a duel with Porus' brother, Amar, where he lost his favourite horse. This shook Alexander. He took another horse to continue the war. Before this, the Macedonians didn't allow any king to even come close to Alexander. Alexander somehow recovered from the shock and found Porus approaching him this time on a horse. They had a severe duel, which lasted for a long time. Alexander's strength was nowhere close to Porus. He fell off his horse. Porus jumped off the horse, went to the fallen emperor and placed a spear on Alexander's throat. Alexander asked him for mercy, but before Porus could think of anything, Alexander's commander attacked Porus and diverted his attention. Before Alexander could regain his composure, a big arrow from one of Porus' commander's bow struck his chest directly. He fell on the ground and lost the grip on his sword. Alexander's body was swamped in a pool of blood; he was unable to stand by himself and became unconscious.

Alexander's bodyguard saw what happened to the Greek king. He rushed towards his master and rescued him back to the camp. He came back to consciousness after a few days after the war got over, causing a big loss on both sides. A large number of brave soldiers lost their lives. The war was stopped as both armies didn't have much left to fight with. The small Paurava Kingdom took on the strongest king in the world. Alexander's aim of reaching the end of the world remained unachieved. He could just depute Greek generals to govern the provinces, which he had won in North-West India.

After Porus, there was a skilful and powerful Nanda Empire with 200,000 infantry, 80,000 cavalry, 8,000 war chariots and 6,000 fighting elephants. Alexander could not even think of war with such a big empire as it would be a suicide attempt. Hence, he decided to return. The ambitious and nasty king, Alexander, had won every battle before he entered India. He died in Babylon in 323 BC three years after the Indian expedition as the wound on his chest from the war with Porus never healed. Porus, the fearless king of India, saved his kingdom and country from invasion. Porus was the first protector of our land from aggressors.

The First Emperor of India

"People's happiness should be King's happiness. The Welfare of people is King's welfare. For a king, there is no task which is only individualistic and pleasurable to him only. It is king's utmost duty to look after the progress and welfare of people of his country."

– Chanakya Niti

"The external threat is approaching towards India. We need to unite under one ruler and fight against the enemy. I request you, my Lord, to leave the secure zone and unite our country, which is fragmented into numerous *Janpadas* and *Mahajanpadas* (small independent kingdoms). If these small kingdoms join Alexander, who is coming in full force from the North-West of our country, then our sovereignty, our culture can be endangered." Chanakya explained the situation to Dhananada, the emperor of Magadha whose empire extended from Bihar in Eastern India to the Indus river in the West.

Dhananada looked at Chanakya, and with a lot of arrogance, replied, "Oh you stupid ugly Brahmin! You are an unaware bugger. You must teach ancient texts to the people. You just focus on your duties; don't poke your nose anywhere else. These political decisions and strategies are not your things."

Chanakya, saddened by the king's reply, joined his hand in *Namaskar mudra* and said, "I request you from my heart. Please save our country. Integrity should be maintained in the country. Alexander is very cruel and inhuman. He has destroyed many kingdoms and religions. Protect us from facing a similar kind of fate." Dhananada became red with anger on hearing this and ordered the guards to punish Chanakya.

Chanakya asked them to stop and spoke angrily, "Oh king, enough of your disdainful behaviour! I pledge today to save my country from any external threat, and also I will make sure you and the Nanda Empire get destroyed completely," and he stormed out.

Chanakya (Kautilya) knew that Dhananada didn't have a single quality required for a king. Only because he was heir to the throne, he was ruling the Nanda Empire. Dhananada (*Dhana* = money) got his name because of his greed for money. He was not liked by his subjects because of his unjust behaviour. This was a very crucial time for India as the Greeks were approaching and the country needed a king who could save the boundaries from the invaders and also keep people happy under his rule. *Ramrajya* (ideal kingdom) was to be established. Chanakya was in search of a man who prioritised the country's needs over self-desires; one who was mighty in strength and lives for the meek.

Chanakya was a teacher at Takshshila University in the North-West region of India. He used to teach Economics and Political Science at the university. In this university, there was a student named Chandragupta, who was very sharp, smart, brave and famous among his batchmates for his shrewdness and intelligence. Chandragupta was born to a *dassi* (slave) of King Dhananada in 340 BC. Chanakya noticed this boy and was impressed by him. He took various physical and mental assessments of Chandragupta. He passed all of them. Kautilya made up his mind and decided to train Chandragupta to make him the saviour of the land from all possible threats. The coming together of Chandragupta and Chanakya changed the course of Indian history.

Chanakya, originally known as Vishnugupta or Kautilya, was not just a teacher in a university but was also an amazing war strategist. He had made up his mind that he won't just make Chandragupta the king of Magadha but also the king of Bharatvarsha. With Chandragupta, he started taking necessary steps for this. He asked Chandragupta to build a strong army, which contained brave and daredevil soldiers. Chandragupta found people who were not happy with the present king Dhananada and requested them to assist his soldiers. Chanakya, in the meanwhile, created unrest among the people of the Nanda Empire as an action against the king. Since what citizens thought about the king was important, he ensured that the people's sentiments were against Dhananada and in favour of Chandragupta.

Chandragupta started approaching Magadha (in Bihar). He, instead of defeating the small kingdoms on his way, pursued them to join hands for the better cause and made them partners in his venture. They accepted Chandragupta as their king after observing his valour and leadership qualities. Many battles took place between the Nanda army and Chandragupta's army. Chandragupta was not always victorious. Sometimes the defeat was massive, but since the determination was strong, bouncing back was not very difficult.

Chanakya and Chandragupta planned another strategy and marched with might and courage towards Magadha. This time, the strike was stronger, and Nanda's army was completely defeated by Chandragupta's army. Dhananada tried to escape when he came to know that he was losing the battle, but it was too late by then. His misery and selfish deeds must have flashed before his eyes when he faced death in the form of defeat from Chandragupta. If he had listened to the prescient Chanakya's request for a united India, this terrible moment would not have come in his life. Chanakya was not asking anything for himself but for the people of India.

He got trapped in the Chakravyuha led by Chanakya and was killed in the hands of Chandragupta. Chandragupta won the war. He was enthroned as the king of Magadha by his Guru, Chanakya, in the year 321 BC. Patliputra was declared the capital of the Empire. A 19-year-old became the king of the land. Chandragupta's mother's name was Mura. Hence, the kingdom was named after her as the Maurya kingdom. Needless to say, he appointed Chanakya as his prime minister.

The first thing Chandragupta and Chanakya did after establishing Maurya rule was that they started building a strong army. For any kingdom to be powerful, the boundaries should be safe and secure. If the army of the nation is weak, its culture, traditions and mannerisms get destroyed. In a matter of just four to five years, the Maurya Empire built a large, fierce army and a strong navy. This army assured people that they were safe under the rule of Chandragupta. Many small kingdoms accepted the sovereignty of Chandragupta. The Maurya Empire spread to the boundaries of present-day Afghanistan. The Maurya Empire had 600,000 infantry, 30,000 cavalries, 2,000 war elephants and 4,000 chariots. With such large army power, Chandragupta was ready to take on any external threat. By the year 315 BC, Chandragupta was confident enough to confront the mighty Macedonians.

This was the time when the area around Kandahar, i.e., Afghanistan was ruled by Alexander's Governor, Seleucus Nicator. When Alexander left India, he appointed different satrapies. Satrapies were governors who ruled a particular province. Chandragupta's armed forces killed two governors, Nicator and Philip, during battles between them. The satrapies like Eudemus and Peithon also fought against the Mauryas with different strategies, but they too were defeated. They left the territories and went back to their own country. After Alexander, Seleucus Nicator brought the whole of Alexander's territory including Babylon under his rule since there were no strong satrapies left. He was the best among all the satrapies and was fearless. With the increased power, he initiated a struggle with Chandragupta Maurya's army as he felt that he had enough power to challenge Chandragupta.

He demanded some regions under Chandragupta, which were won by Alexander during his Indian expedition. Seleucus was not aware that it was a new India under the rule of a new brave emperor. This empire now belonged to Chandragupta and the kingmaker, Chanakya, the cleverest individual of all time.

Chandragupta not only ignored the demands of Seleucus but also asked for provinces of Afghanistan under Seleucus' dominance. Chanakya told the Greeks that the Afghanistan land is a part of the Indian subcontinent and any outsider had no business possessing the regions. Hearing this, Seleucus got provoked and decided to head towards the Mauryan Empire for war. This was Seleucus' biggest mistake; he could not have expected what was coming his way.

Chandragupta and his army were ready for the war. A massive war broke out between the Greeks and Indians, which continued for days. Seleucus applied all his efforts to win the war, but when Maurya had a king who was an amazing fighter himself, the victory was obvious for the Mauryans. Seleucus didn't have an option but to surrender as there was a severe loss of his army. He withdrew from the war, but it was not yet over for the opponent; Chanakya demanded that Seleucus gave away the area from Gandhar to the Hindu Kush, i.e., present-day Afghanistan, back to India for the war to end. The Greeks, without any discussion, decided to give in to all the demands made by the Indians. They understood that maintaining cordial relations with Indians would be beneficial for them.

Seleucus Nicator was sure by now that he too should have an ally like that of Chandragupta. He felt he could take Chandragupta's help to win the war in the Western areas of the Greek kingdom. He agreed to all the terms of Maurya and also married his daughter to Chandragupta as a gesture of peace. As part of the treaty, Chandragupta accepted the offer and also gave 500 war elephants to the Greeks in return. These elephants proved to be of great help to Seleucus in his further battles against the enemies of the Western part of the Greek kingdom. After Seleucus, not a single European power tried to invade India for the next 1,500 years.

This victory made Chandragupta the emperor of India. Except for a few kingdoms like Kalinga and those kingdoms from down South like Chola, Pandya, Keralputra and Satiyaputra, the rest of India was under Maurya's rule. This was the golden era in Indian history. Peace prevailed among all kingdoms. The king was selfless and for the people. The boundaries were safe and secure. Chandragupta was the real great emperor and the perfect individual in a true sense. He built the whole kingdom out of nothing. The son of a slave became the emperor of India. Chanakya was his only help. He ruled the Indian subcontinent for a couple of years, and in 298 BC, he renounced everything and accepted Jainism. He performed his duty as per Chanakya's guidelines and gave away his empire to his son, Bindusara, and he became a monk. He requested Chanakya to stay with Bindusara to help him take India to new heights. Ashoka succeeded Bindusara in the Maurya dynasty. During his reign, the

Mauryan Empire reached Iran in the West up to Bengal in the East.

At its peak, the Maurya Empire was the largest and the most populous empire in the world, dwarfing both Alexander's domains and those of Shi Huangdi in China. For the first time, India saw awareness of the whole subcontinent as a geographical and civilisational unit, and Indian civilisation was already well-developed and conscious. Everyone flourished a lot. Maurya connected the whole subcontinent by good roads. *Uttara path* (Grand trunk road) was a well-built route by the Mauryan emperors. This route was further used for trade and business by every ruling king of India. Even in British rule, the British concretised this road for vehicles. The Mauryan emperors exchanged ambassadors and trade delegations with Alexander's successors in the Middle East.

One should not forget that the fate achieved by the Mauryan emperors had a large contribution from Chanakya and his *Arthashastra*. Also, the administration and laws for the empire were set by Chanakya himself, which were also stated in the *Arthashastra*. He was the first to keep the idea of central governance with one king in the centre, who will be responsible for allocating governors of different regions. Further down, he wanted the local government to have bodies that could administrate even smaller areas. Different people were assigned at different levels like Chief armed forces, Minister, Town Manager, Treasurer, Commander, Junior Officer, etc. This idea is used by almost all countries in the world today.

The First Emperor of India

Arthashastra tells us about the different duties of every responsible individual from king to a junior officer. Foreign policies were also a major part of Kautilya's *Arthashastra*. *Arthashastra* also has a long list of laws speaking about the civic sense during Mauryan rule. For example, traffic rules stated that bullock carts were not allowed to move without a driver, a child can only drive a cart if accompanied by an adult, etc. Reckless driving was punished. Even present-day India has taken large inspiration from the Mauryan rule. The Mauryan lions and the *chakra* became the country's national symbol. India inherited many qualities as a nation from the first emperor of India and from his Guru who united the country in a true sense.

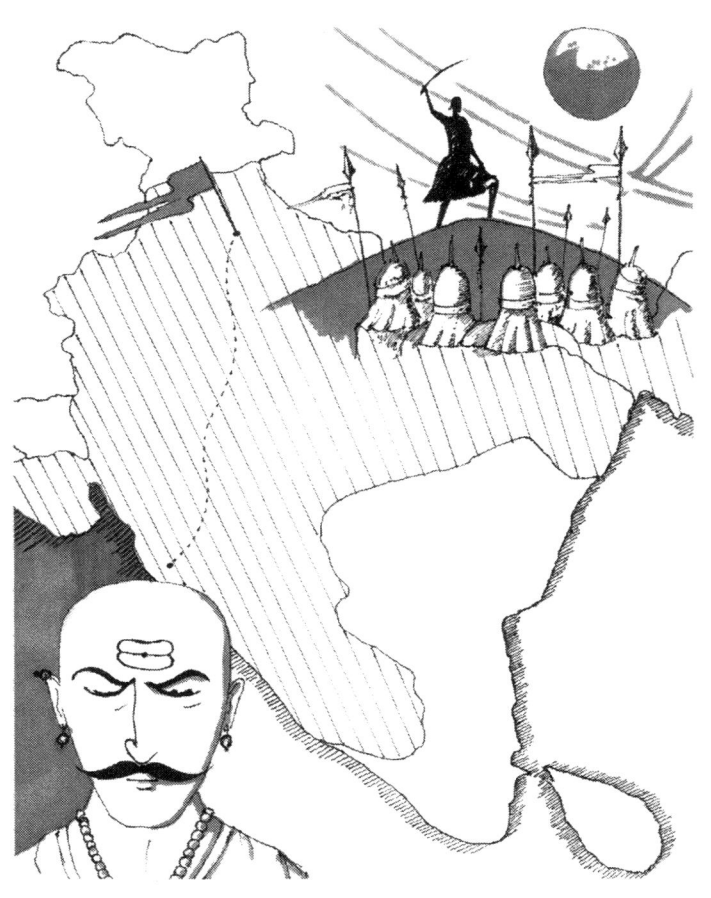

Battle of Delhi

"Diye huye vachan ke liye… satya aur nyay ke liye… dharam stapana ke liye… kisi ke bhi virudh jaana pade, woh chahe parmatma hi kyun na ho… toh bhaybheet na ho… yahi dharam hai, yahi kshatriya dharam hai." (For the promises that have been made… for truth and justice… for the establishment of righteousness… if you have to go against anyone, even if that's supreme power… then don't fear that… since that is duty; the duty of a warrior.)

– Dialogue from *Baahubali*

I have visited Shanivar Wada many times since my childhood. Now the great monument has a simple standing structure though there is some attraction alive. This glorious structure has a place in every Pune resident's heart. I remember the day when I visited Shanivar Wada with my father. I had just finished my board exam. On one normal day, my father and I decided to explore a few places in Pune. We made our first halt at Shanivar Wada. The environment around the Wada was no different than any other monument in India. There were guides to tell us about the historical importance, hawkers selling photos of Shanivar Wada and photographers to click some candid photos.

We clicked a few snaps and selfies outside the gate and entered the premises. The walls of the Wada were sturdy and rugged. My father had great interest and information about the Maratha Empire, which he started sharing with me. He told me how Shivaji Maharaj built the kingdom by winning forts and later turned it into a huge empire. He asked me a few questions related to Shivaji Maharaj, which I answered correctly as I was aware of the Maratha king. I thanked my history textbooks and many serials shown on television. Then my father pointed to the statue of Bajirao Peshwa, which was standing tall at the entrance of Shanivar Wada and asked me if I knew something about that man. My answer came out from the knowledge I had received from a commercial box office hit celluloid. He was thunderstruck after hearing my pitiable knowledge. He then decided to enlighten me about the great Maratha warrior, Bajirao Ballal. Till that day, Peshwa Bajirao Ballal for me was just a name printed on one of the pages of my history textbook. My little knowledge from the cinema told me that he was a lover who went against the Hindu regulations to marry a Muslim princess, Mastani. My father had something very different in his eyes for the great warrior.

He narrated to me many facts and stories of Bajirao's life. Bajirao was one of the finest warriors this country has ever seen. The story that my father narrated to me that day was the story of the Delhi battle—a story of bravery and extreme audacity.

Bajirao Ballal was appointed the (Peshwa) Major General of Chhatrapati Shahu's kingdom at the age of twenty after the demise of his father, Balaji Vishwanath. He gained immense popularity in the Maratha Kingdom. He vexed Mughals, Nizams and Rajputs by conquering their forts and territories. He was 6 feet tall with a lean physique. He had a radiant face and thick handlebar moustache.

He had a single dream of bringing the whole of Hindustan back into the power of Indians. The invaders had destroyed the life of the local people. They turned riches into rages. Indians were denied every basic aspect of life. Muhamad Shah Rangila was the Mughal emperor during Bajirao's reign. The old but witty emperor was cruel like his ancestors. Malharrao Holkar was one of the generals of the Maratha Empire who tried to attack Delhi to dethrone the Mughal emperor. Hearing the news, Muhamad Shah asked his General, Sadad Ali Khan, to fight the incoming troops. There was a fierce battle between Holkar's army and Sadad Ali's army. But unfortunately things didn't go as planned for the Marathas, and hence, they had to withdraw from the battlefield. The Marathas faced considerable loss in this battle. Muhamad Shah made up a story that Bajirao Peshwa had lost the battle. He tried to create a perception among the people that the Marathas who were considered as saviours had lost. This shattered people's hope of *Swarajya* (Independent Rule) being restored. They saw a ray of hope in Bajirao for better and peaceful living. But if he lost against the evil Delhi

Sultanate, then the civilians would have no one to look forward to.

This news reached Shanivar Wada. Bajirao got extremely annoyed and decided to castigate the Mughals. He reached out to his best 500 cavalry regiment and said that they needed to do something massive and act to ensure that the people regain their trust back in them.

One soldier asked him, "Peshwa, what do you mean by something massive?"

Peshwa smiled and replied, "We must attack Delhi."

All the soldiers supported Bajirao's decision. Everyone was waiting for this day to come. Everyone from this land between the Himalayan ranges and the Indian Ocean saw the dream to live in Swarajya and see a just and kind-hearted king on the Delhi throne. Everybody got charged up and started to prepare for the most courageous battle of their lives. The army prepared themselves physically and mentally. Peshwa, with his army, studied the strengths and weaknesses of the enemy. Bajirao was of the firm belief that soldiers should sweat more during peace, which is better than to bleed in war. All the 500 men with Peshwa Bajirao had sleepless nights and thought only about the best technique and strategy to be implemented against Mughals in the war.

A day for the epic battle was decided, and everything was set. On March 25, 1737, Bajirao, with his brave army, started the march towards Delhi from Pune. The distance between Pune and Delhi is 1,500 kilometres approximately. During those times when the fastest mode of transport was horseback, the distance was usually covered in ten days. Bajirao was famous due to his special modus operandi for war. He used a method called the *Blitzkrieg* method. In this method, the army marched towards the enemy with tremendous speed. This puzzled the enemy with the estimation of the arrival time of Bajirao's army. Bajirao, along with his troops, reached Delhi in merely 48 hours.

The brave and fully charged up army didn't stop for rest during the whole voyage. On 28th March, Bajirao attacked Delhi with a terrific force. The Mughal emperor got terrified hearing the news that Bajirao had come to seize Delhi. He ordered his best troopers to fight against the Marathas. Muhamad Shah sent the army of more than 100,000 men. It was a matter of life and death for the Mughal emperor. He used all his strength against the Marathas. But this time his enemy was none other than the bravest leader of the 18th century, Bajirao Peshwa, who managed to unite his army with the army of Malharrao Holkar, increasing the strength of the Maratha soldiers exponentially.

Bajirao defeated the Mughal army in a matter of two days. He left no time for the emperor to plot and execute against the Marathas. On 31st March, he surrounded the Red Fort and asked Muhammad Shah to surrender immediately as an ultimatum to the Mughal emperor. After 550 years of a long wait, a Hindu king or a king from this land won a major battle in Delhi. Muhammad Shah, with his trusted officer, hid in the Delhi Fort.

Muhammad Shah tried all his ways to escape from the hands of Marathas and sought every way to retaliate. He even tried to bribe the Maratha officials, but they were so loyal to Bajirao that they couldn't even think of betraying their leader.

Hence, Muhammad Shah failed miserably in all his attempts to save himself. Finally, he surrendered to Bajirao. According to Marathas' rules and benevolent culture set by Shivaji Maharaj, if an enemy is ready to surrender, then one should forgive him and not punish him. The kind-hearted Bajirao followed the same set of norms. He just made sure that the wrong perception created by Mughals, which was among the civilians about the Maratha's earlier defeat must diminish. The news of Bajirao's victory comforted everybody. On his return journey towards Pune, his army consisted of 80,000 men.

The story was not over yet. When Bajirao's army was about to reach Bhopal, they came across an annoying and surprising piece of news. They found that the Nizam of Hyderabad and Nawab of Bhopal were heading with a large army towards Delhi. They were asked for help by Mughals when Bajirao was approaching Delhi. But the speed of Peshwa was so fast that by now the Nizam had just managed to reach halfway that is Bhopal. The Nizam issued a war cry against the Marathas in Bhopal. He thought that their total army would be enough to overpower Bajirao's army. There were more than 175,000 men. Bajirao first tried to settle the situation peacefully.

It is well-known that war means heavy loss of human lives. It was always taught in Indian culture since *Ramayana* that we should first offer the enemy to settle the grievances without engaging in war. If the enemy is adamant and not ready to submit, then one should go for war. This is the sign of a really brave warrior. The courageous General, Bajirao, decided to fight against the armies. The battle was called the Battle of Bhopal. This ferocious battle was considered to be the biggest battle fought by Bajirao. Many soldiers died from both sides. Bajirao's army succeeded in crushing the attack of massive armies. They won with a big margin though there was a big loss of property, animals and men.

Bajirao didn't let the Nizam go easily. He was already warned once by Bajirao that he shouldn't help the Mughals against the Marathas, but the Nizam didn't keep his words. Bajirao asked for some territories which were under the Nizam's rule to be annexed by Chhatrapati Shahu. He asked for Malwa, the fertile area of the river Narmada and also some regions of Chambal and the adjoining areas. This was a major setback for the Nizam of Hyderabad. It broke the spine of the mighty Nizamshahi. The rapacity of the Nizam cost him a huge price. Bajirao did not even spare the Nawab of Bhopal. He was fined a sum of 5,000,000 to make up for the expenses incurred during the war. The Nawab had no other option but to give away the money to Bajirao. These two major wars increased the power of the Maratha Empire.

Bajirao returned to Pune, which was lit in blissfulness. People celebrated the victory just like Diwali. Shanivar Wada was lit with *diyas*. Shivaji Maharaj started establishing Swarajya in the year 1646 from the Torna Fort to create *Hindavi Swarajya*. By the end of the year 1737, a large number of Indian territories were under the Maratha Empire. During the tenure of Bajirao, provinces from Afghanistan to Bengal and from Punjab to Karnataka were under the Maratha Empire. The saffron flag was waving with utmost pride. Bajirao turned Swarajya (Independent rule) into *Samrajya* (Empire). The Maratha power increased so much after that that they remained the only powerful help for the Delhi Sultanate from external invasions. Marathas became the real rulers of India. Muhammad Shah was only a ruler for namesake. He was just a puppet in the hands of the Maratha rulers.

When Nadir Shah, a cruel king who was ruling near the Northwestern borders of India tried to attack Delhi, Muhammad Shah asked for the immediate help of Bajirao to save his life. Nadir Shah destroyed the Non-Islamic properties like temples, universities and other cultural monuments during his march towards Delhi. Marathas and Mughals stopped Nadir Shah's army from harming India. Bajirao saved India from a fanatic who was trying to enthrone himself as the emperor of India. Bajirao's contribution is very important in Indian history. He fought forty huge wars in a matter of just 20 years of his tenure. He didn't lose a single war. No matter what the size of the enemy was, he won the battles and expanded the Maratha Empire.

I heard the story with tremendous excitement and goosebumps. My chest filled with pride. I was so ignorant of the splendid courage of the great Peshwa Bajirao. Then I looked at Bajirao's statue, and this time, it appeared brighter and stronger to me.

Vishwavidyalaya

"The purpose of education is to make good human beings with skill and expertise. Enlightened human beings can be created by teachers."

– A. P. J. Abdul Kalam

My brother, Sudhakar Patil, once shared an amazing experience he had when he visited China. He was studying in a reputed business school in India where he got an opportunity to opt for the student exchange programme and went to China to study different subjects for a couple of months. He met a fellow student named Wang Lee during the visit. They became very good friends, and as typical friends, they used to study together. They had many common interests. One day, they were studying together in the institute's library, and they were discussing the Indian and Chinese education systems. Wang told Sudhakar that the Chinese education system had subjects that have certain topics about the glorious universities of India.

Sudhakar was surprised and asked him, "How is it possible? In India, we barely have a history of colleges or universities. Traditionally, a teacher used to sit under a banyan tree and teach some Brahmin students. The educational system of India took shape after our independence in 1947."

Wang replied, "Have you ever heard of the names like Takshashila, Nalanda and Vikramshila universities?"

Sudhakar had a big question mark on his face. He said, "But these are some monuments, which are there in India, and we had very little to study about them in our history textbooks, how come they are in your textbooks?" By that time, Wang understood that Sudhakar knew very little about the universities that shaped many Indian and Chinese generations from the past. Wang closed the book that he was reading and started telling facts that changed Sudhakar's perspective about India and India's contribution to the academic field. Wang began sharing the knowledge that he had to which Sudhakar listened very patiently with attention.

Wang said, "Takshashila and Nalanda were the biggest and oldest universities in India. Takshashila was established around 2,700 years ago. It was built around the fifth century BC. It is located in Pakistan presently and is called Taxila. Students from all over the world competed among themselves to get admission at Takshashila University. The affluent kingdoms, empires and nations used to send their best cadres to Takshashila. Iraq, Greece, Egypt, Syria, Turkey, Arabia, and even China were the main countries that sent students to study in Takshashila. The entrance exam was so tough that only one-third of the applicants would crack the exam. The minimum age of admission in this institute was sixteen. One needed to be well-versed by that age in many subjects to get into this *Vishwavidyalaya*.

Many students had to leave their homes to study at this university. The questions for the entrance exam were very difficult, consisting of material, physical as well as questions from the spiritual genre. The syllabus was mostly influenced by the concepts from Hinduism, Buddhism, and Jainism. The subjects for studies were from all walks of life. The study made the students a perfect character, one who could earn bread and also spend one's life elegantly. The university taught the students about thinking for the welfare of society. The main subjects taught were Vedic Philosophy, Languages, Astronomy, Astrology, Commerce, and Futurology."

Sudhakar stopped Wang and asked, "What is Futurology and how come Astronomy was taught 2,700 years ago? Are you joking, Wang? European countries were the pioneers to study and learn astronomy. They imparted to the world knowledge about the sun, stars, planets and other celestial objects."

Wang smiled and replied, "No, Sudhakar, I am not kidding at all. Futurology is a study of postulating possible, probable and preferable futures. Somewhat like that of forecasting the outcomes. Astronomy was studied and understood by Indians long back before the Europeans and Indians taught astronomy to the world much before anyone else. The solar and lunar eclipse, full moon (*Poornima*) and new moon (*Amavasya*) days and their significance are present in the sacred *Vedas*. *Shulba Sutras* is a very famous text dedicated to constructions discussing advanced mathematics and astronomy. Also, there is an episode in the *Vedas* called *Vedanga Jyotisha,* which tells us about astronomy and astrology. You Indians knew the best time to initiate and celebrate an auspicious occasion. By the end of the fifth century, India knew before anyone else that the sun is stationary and the earth revolves around the sun. You should feel proud of this, my friend."

Sudhakar was pleasantly surprised to know all these facts. Wang Lee continued, "So these were the subjects taught in the university. But these were to understand the theoretical concepts. Also, self-defence and protecting others too is important, which is why archery and warfare techniques were also major subjects in the curriculum. Music and dance were the art forms taught in this Vishwavidyalaya. The main significance of the university was that everyone was free to learn their favourite subjects. The limited seats were a foreign concept during that period.

The teachers of this university were also very experienced and genius in their respective subjects. They made sure that every student becomes an expert in his or her choice of subject. The great Chanikya was one of them." Sudhakar giggled after hearing the pronunciation of Chanakya made by Wang.

Sudhakar corrected Wang and said, "It is not Chanikya, it is Chanakya, also known as Kautilya (Vishnugupta was his real name). We, Indians, are very proud of him. Even today, we call him the most brilliant and highly diplomatic individuals as Chanakya. The kingmakers in Indian politics are called Chanakya. He wrote *Arthashastra*, which is still the principal text for every Economics and Political Science student. Anyway, what did he teach in Takshashila?"

Wang replied, "Yes, you are right, Sudhakar! He was a teacher of Political Science and Economics in Takshashila. Takshashila was very famous because of its prominent and prodigious alumni. It is said that the great emperor, Chandragupta Maurya, was a student of this esteemed university, who then ruled the land of seven rivers, your country, India. It was the largest Indian empire of all times.

Have you read *Panchatantra* stories by any chance?"

Sudhakar immediately replied, "Yes! It is a collection of amazing animal fables with moral values. My childhood bedtime stories from *Panchtantra* were recited to me by my granny."

Wang replied, "Did you know that the creator of *Panchatantra* was an alumnus of this Vishwavidyalaya. His name was Vishnu Sharma. *Panchatantra* is the most translated Indian literary product of India. This book has 200 versions in more than fifty languages. *Arabian Nights*, *Aesop's Fables*, *Sindbad* and many such interesting and entertaining stories were inspired from Panchatantra. Such stories are found to be entertaining for the children even today. *Jataka tales* of Sri Lanka were also motivated by Vishnu Sharma's work. Such immortal work was done by the graduates of Takshashila.

You would like to hear that even the great Charaka, the father of Ayurveda, was also a student of this reputed university. He is known as the 'Indian father of medicine'. He wrote a book called *Charaka Samhita*, which is used as one of the significant textbooks in present-day medical colleges. Alexander was astonished to see the literary wealth of Takshashila when he witnessed such extraordinarily intelligent students. He took some of the scholars from Takshashila back with him when he returned after trailing in India. *Gandhar* art, which is one of the most famous forms of art, had its roots in Takshashila. The idols of Lord Buddha that we see today was the creation of Gandhar art form. Lord Buddha had visited this campus many times. There was a place made for Gautama to stay when he used to come to the campus to guide the contemporary batch. Gautama Buddha looks so mesmerising and calm in such a piece of art. Doesn't he?"

Sudhakar said, "Yes. Thanks to Takshashila students! It is because of them that Buddha became animate for us and more understandable. When you have an idol in front of you, your spiritual connection with the Supreme is easier.

I have one question. How come you know so much about Takshashila though not being an Indian?"

Wang smiled and said, "As the university was so attractive to knowledge seekers, many Chinese monks like Faxian and Hue en Tsang travelled to Takshashila and gained knowledge. They brought many books and records with them to China. After that, many such monks continued the trend. This knowledge got assimilated into our culture and has been passed on to many generations. We respect the Indian universities so much that even the Chinese government has established a university named Nanhai, inspired by the biggest and largest Indian University called Nalanda."

Sudhakar asked Wang in pride, "Was Nalanda even bigger than Takshashila? I know it was somewhere in Bihar but don't know much about it. Do you have any important information about Nalanda University?"

Wang took a sip of water and said, "Yes, my brother! Nalanda was the largest university in the world in terms of area and many other parameters. The entire campus was spread across an area of 15,000,000 square metres. It was a residential Vishwavidyalaya. It was the first of its kind. Students used to spend three years of their life in the Nalanda campus. It consisted of eleven big Hindu temples and many Buddhist stupas. The ancient Nalanda University was believed to be built during the rule of the Gupta dynasty. The king, Kumargupta, built the university probably in the fifth century AD. Nalanda University was open for pupils in the period from the fifth century to the twelfth century. It became a renowned college in the world in the ninth century.

The campus was so huge that 10,000 students used to study in a single academic year, and there were 2,000 qualified teachers to teach them. Hence, if you see the teacher-to-student ratio, it was very less, and therefore, there was appropriate knowledge transfer from the tutor to the pupil. Like that of Takshashila, even in Nalanda, the students came to study from all over the world. Tibet, China, Persia, Nepal, Greece, Turkey and Sri Lanka are some of the nations that used to send the students to Nalanda. The peculiarity of this university was that the students had to follow Buddhism by changing their attire and shaving off their heads before getting into the college so that they could focus more on studies and be less distracted. But after they passed out of college, they had the option to follow their religions. Many subjects like that of Takshashila were studied here by the students. They also learnt tantric and Indian logic. Do you know what Indian logic is? I don't have much insight into it."

Sudhakar thought for a while and said, "Yes, Indian logic is like a means of knowledge. Along with the five senses, we have been given some very crucial things by the Almighty. That is called *Pramanas*. Pramanas has six groups *Pratyaksha* (Direct perception by sense contact), *Anumana* (Inference), *Sabda* (Verbal testimony of *Vedas*), *Upamana* (Examples), *Arthapatti* (conjecture of insignificant information) and *Anupalabdhi* (absence of a particular thing).

Wang nodded and said, "Thank you for the information. Such in-depth and significant information was available at Nalanda University. The campus had three huge libraries named Ratna Sagar, Ratno Devi and Ratna Vanjak. They were nine-floor building structures. They consisted of around 9,000,000 books of different subjects from astronomy to medicine.

The students were divided into three categories according to merit and got subjects accordingly. The notable scholars who studied at Nalanda University included Harshavardhana, Vasubandhu, Dharmapala, Suvishnu, Asanga, Dharmakirti, Nagarjuna, Padmasambhava, Xuanzang and Hwui Li. These stalwarts were significant in their respective fields. The generations understood many things only because of these scholars' contributions. But above all, the man who gave so much to the world in mathematics and astronomy, Aryabhatta, was the student of this prestigious Vishwavidyalaya. He taught the world to count; he enlightened the world about the celestial objects. Sudhakar, this is all I know about these two greatest abodes of knowledge.

There were many such institutes in India like Vikramshila, Ujjan, etc. The students from these Vishwavidyalayas became monks and showed the world a proper direction to lead a better life or worked in a king's court and guided him in the maintenance of the kingdom and for the welfare of the society.

C'mon man! Let's study now, enough of my sermon."

Wang opened his book again to study. But Sudhakar was in a different world, thinking about his country. He held his mobile in his hand and started staring at the wallpaper, which had a picture of him saluting the Indian tricolour.

Mighty Vijaynagaram

"While Ram was ruling the kingdom, there were happy families, with no widows to lament, no danger from wild animals, nor any fear born of diseases.

Every creature was full of joy and happiness. Everyone was engaged in the pursuit of dharmic actions or virtue. Turning their eyes towards Rama alone, creatures did not kill one another.

All the people were endowed with excellent characteristics. All were engaged in dharma."

– Sage Valmiki in *Yuddha Kanda* of *Ramayana*

Everyone around the world is aware that ancient India was called the 'Golden Sparrow'. It was titled so because this land of India was wealthy, prosperous and had established socio-economic systems. India's GDP share was approximately 28% of the world's GDP during the pre-Islam invasion era. It was roughly 23% when the British invaded India. After that, the downfall of the country's economy started rapidly. In the year 2011, India contributed 3.9% of the world's GDP.

In the last 2,500 years, this land attracted kings, rulers and traders from around the world. From Arabs to Turks, from Mongols to Mahmud, and the Portuguese to the British tried to invade India to earn money or to spread their religion. Every traveller came to this land and wrote about the richness of the land. The richness of the land was in terms of economy, literature and spirituality. India was exporting raw material as well as finished products. All these products enjoyed a worldwide demand.

India was called the 'land of spices' by outsiders, but it was not only about spices. Bharat had a long list of other stuff like cotton, iron, textiles, pearls, sugar, etc. to offer to the world. India was the major exporter of many such items. India's import was nominal in comparison to the huge export. There were some sovereign states in Africa, which banned trade with India because the value of Indian currency increased tremendously in their state and value for the native currency decreased, which triggered economic instability in those nations. India had diverse weather conditions. Such conditions suited a large variety of crops. Eventually, cultivation of a wide range of raw materials and manufacturing of finished products was possible in India. Many Indian cities had some speciality in various products, and those products were in high demand in the international market. For example, shawls and carpets from Kashmir and Amritsar, silk sarees of Varanasi and silk cloth of Nagpur. Such variety brought a huge amount of capital to this land. One can visualise the kind of humongous wealth shown in the magnum opus *Baahubali* series. All the prosperity pictured in the movie was a bright reality during that period in India. One such empire that illustrates all the mentioned prosperity was the Vijaynagar Empire.

This is a tale that exemplifies the magnificence and grandeur of a majestic Empire of India. The Vijaynagar Empire was in existence from the fourteenth century to the seventeenth century. It was one of the largest empires ruled by Hindu kings. The whole of South India was under Vijayanagar rule.

Vijaynagar was ruled by many dynasties for four centuries. It was established by Harihara and Bukka. They were the disciples of saint Vidyaranya. He was the 12th Jagadguru of the *Sringeri Sarada Pitham* (Sringeri Sharada Peetham was one of the four Vedanta monasteries (matha) established by Adi Shankaracharya around 800 AD in Sringeri (Karnataka), the others being Dwaraka (Gujarat), Jagannath Puri (Odisha) and Jyotirmath (Uttarakhand)) from years 1380–1386. Both were commanders of King Kakatiya of Warangal (in Telangana).

Mohammed bin Tuglaq was ruling Delhi during that period. He attacked Warangal with a large army and defeated King Kakatiya. Both Harihara and Bukka, along with many other soldiers, were prisoners of the war. They were taken to Delhi and were forcefully converted to Islam. They were asked to serve the royal court and were appointed as the governors of the Delhi Sultanate. They were sent to different provinces to win over the unconquered kingdoms. During one such expedition to South India, they met their Guru, Vidyaranya. He was meditating in one ashram. Sage Vidyaranya immediately recognised his pupils though they were in Islamic outfits.

He blessed them and said, "One day, you will be the emperor of this land."

But Harihara said, "It is no longer possible. We are slaves of Delhi. We don't have the freedom to have such dreams."

Vidyaranya smiled and replied, "Life is not over, my son. You can again come back to the correct path."

He convinced both and converted them back into Hinduism. Then with the support of Sage Vidyaranya, Harihara and Bukka built a powerful Hindu army and further founded the Vijaynagar kingdom. It was called

Vidyanagar initially during those days. Sangama Dynasty of Harihara continued to rule the kingdom henceforth. Many kings like Bukka, Deva Raya, Virupaksha, Mallikarjuna and Pradhu ruled Vidyanagar after Harihara's reign.

The kingdom earned the name Vijaynagar as its army was winning many battles continuously. Vijaynagar was forming a strong kingdom with respect to its military and wealth. It was surrounded by many gruesome enemies like Bahamani, Sultans of Bijapur, Golconda and Delhi. During the end of the fifteenth century, the reigns of Vijaynagar were under the Tuluva Dynasty. This middle-sized kingdom became a superpower empire under the reign of emperor Krishnadevaraya from the same Tuluva Dynasty. The Vijaynagar Empire was at the apex in every field during Krishnadevaraya's reign. These are the years from 1509–1529.

The emperor's coronation took place on the birthday of Lord Krishna. This day is considered to be a very auspicious day in the Indian subcontinent. Krishnadevaraya was a tall and well-built man. He was huge in size and had tremendous muscle power. It was famously spoken in the lore that he used to drink a certain amount of oil daily and exercised so heavily until all the oil came out as sweat. He was physically extremely powerful and also mentally very calm and composed. Absolute stillness and ultimate movement were a part of his nature.

A successful empire should have fortified boundaries, everlasting social and religious conditions, and a fast-growing economy. Vijayanagar was on par in all these parameters of being a successful empire. Krishnadevaraya had administrated his kingdom with the help of eight ministers who were called *Ashtadiggajas*. Timmarusu was the prime minister who managed many important portfolios of the empire. Tenali Raman was one of the Ashtadiggajas who was well-known for his wit and wisdom. He helped the king in politics inside and outside the empire. The war strategies and different treaties with neighbouring kingdoms were discussed by the king with Tenali Raman before taking any concrete decisions. Tenali Raman was not only a famous jester in the king's court but also the king's closest adviser. Krishnadevaraya had bright and clever intellectuals around him to guide him. A great leader has a quality; he could hand pick apt people for the posts.

The Vijaynagar Empire under Krishnadevaraya had a huge army. The lore described that the king's personal army consisted of 700,000 infantry, 82,000 cavalrymen, and over 900 elephants. Vijaynagar had 200,000 troops as a reserve army. Such perfect combination of wit and power helped Krishnadevaraya to win battles against many enemies like Muslim kings, Portuguese and other Hindu kings like Gajapati of Orissa. Lodis and then, Mughals were ruling Delhi during the period when the Vijaynagar Empire was ruling the South. More than half of India was suppressed under such foreign rulers. But South India was flourishing under the fair and righteous emperor, Krishnadevaraya. Four major battles took place between Adhilshah and Krishnadevaraya. One of them was the famous Battle of Raichur where Krishnadevaraya's army destroyed Adhilshah's army and pushed them in the north of Krishna River. The mighty elephants of Vijaynagar crushed the *Adilshahi* soldiers. In all the battles, Krishnadevaraya emerged victorious. The same drill happened with Qutubshah's army, and numerous major battles took place with the Bahamanis Sultan too.

Krishnadevaraya knew that the Muslim kings could get along together to fight against the Vijaynagar Empire, so he convinced the Gajapati kingdom to go under the peace treaty with Vijaynagar. He also made sure with the help of his witty ministers and efficient spy team that these Muslim kingdoms didn't join hands and form a team.

Krishnadevaraya was not only an able administrator but also an excellent general. He led his army from the front and even got wounded in some battles. There were some instances where Krishnadevaraya was on the verge of defeat. His army then happened to get disheartened by the loss they might suffer. Krishnadevaraya, then, motivated them with inspiring and encouraging words. A leader should possess oratory skills and a sharp presence of mind. He owned both qualities in him. Such skills helped him to become the emperor of the land.

Krishnadevaraya built a strong navy to safeguard the water borders. He appointed generals to look after the huge coastal line of South India. His strong navy also invaded Sri Lanka and took it under Krishnadevaraya's control. This stronghold on navy also flourished the trade. Because of such tremendous all-round power, Babur, the Mughal emperor, never attacked Vijaynagar. He knew that he could not match the power of Krishnadevaraya. He was cognizant about the result of the wars held between Vijayanagar and Muslim sultanates of the South. Krishnadevaraya was also called the destroyer of Turks.

Such kind of military requires strong economic power. A country can sustain by itself, but to grow as an economic might and to prosper, it should have proper trade relations with its neighbours and also with the outer world. The country should have something distinctive to offer to the world to get the wealth worth relishing in return. As Vijayanagar was a rich empire, many travellers visited and went back to their respective nations. One of them was Fernao Nunes. He had written about many aspects of the Vijayanagar kingdom. He said, "I have never seen or heard of such a wealthy empire in the world." He compared Vijaynagar with Rome. There was rarely any beggar asking for alms in this wealthy empire. Everyone was self-sufficient in their basic necessities. Almost all men or women used to wear golden chains and ornaments. There were ponds full of melted gold. Diamond mines were found in Karnal and Anantapur districts of the Vijayanagar Empire.

Krishnadevaraya established a city named Hampi. It was the richest and most beautiful city in the world. The city had many humongous temples and the Raj Darbar (Royal Court) of Krishnadevaraya. The Hampi city was a state-of-the-art structure. The trade was set up during those times by the emperor. Vijayanagar had trade relations with China, Alexandria, Portugal, South Africa, Persia, Arabia, Maldives and Burma. The Shah of Persia was a close aide to Krishnadevaraya, and the relations between Persia and Vijayanagar were very cordial and based on mutual respect. Many ports were set on the West coast of Vijaynagar. Trade relations with various nations helped him in the battles against his enemies. Like in the fiercest battle against Adhilshah, Vijaynagar used matchlock (one type of a hand cannon), which was bought from the Portuguese. During the reign of Krishnadevaraya, the Portuguese didn't attack any part of India. But they invaded many regions after the emperor's death.

Vijayanagar was a very liberal empire, socially and culturally. Everyone was treated equally in this territory. A learned and an educated king, Krishnadevaraya had written a book in the Telugu language named *Amuktamalyadha*, which sums up his eloquent character.

Many Hindu deities were worshipped by the people of Vijayanagar. Even the emperor himself was a huge devotee of Lord Vithoba. He built a huge temple of Vithoba in Hampi. It was said that Krishnadevaraya requested Vithoba to live in Hampi and not in Pandharpur (place in Maharashtra where the principal temple of Vithoba exists) as the temples in Maharashtra were not very safe under the Muslim rulers. In every battle, Krishnadevaraya carried the idols of many deities with him. He encouraged people to go for pilgrimages in different parts of the country. He, along with his wife, went many times to visit Lord Tirupati in Andhra Pradesh. He had made a provision to keep some amount of the empire's budget for rebuilding and maintenance of temples. There were many picturesque temples in Hampi. South India was protected by such a divine man. Southern India saw some remarkable days under Krishnadevaraya's rule. It was shining bright like a star. Even today, the traditions and culture are followed predominantly in Southern India. One can still see the imprints of Vijaynagar in the life of Indians living in the South. May Lord Krishna bless the entire land called India with many such Krishnadevarayas.

Ahomic War

"I don't believe in taking right decisions. I take decisions and then make them right."

– Ratan Tata

Traditionally when any outsider came to our motherland with an ambition to rule, he forcibly converted the people into his belief systems. He made sure those who were not faithful to his religion would be punished. He used to impose huge taxes, adversities and made the life of people miserable. Destruction of temples by the kings had become a trend during the Delhi Sultanate era. 47,000 temples were destroyed under the rule of Islamic emperors. Many educational institutes were grounded so that the aggressor could propagate his thoughts among his subjects. Very few Hindu kings sustained against such cruel aggressors between the twelfth and eighteenth centuries.

But not all outsiders were wicked. There was a kingdom called the Ahom Kingdom that assimilated into the land's culture. The empire lasted for more than 600 long years. There was barely any other empire that persisted for so long. The Indian state 'Assam' got its name from Ahom. This kingdom ruled in the northeast part of India, which was famously called the 'seven sisters'.

This empire was established by Sukaphaa who came from Eastern Myanmar. He crossed the Patkai hills, which are located in today's Myanmar. He travelled to India with three queens, two sons and with 9,000 trustworthy soldiers. This northeastern land was favourable for wet rice cultivation as the Brahmaputra river basin had ample rainfall, which was a great encouragement for farming. The river is famous till date for floods and has fertile land around it. Sukaphaa reached Kamrup (located in central Assam) on December 2, 1228. He settled towards the southern part of the Brahmaputra river. He requested the local groups like *Marans* and *Barahis* to join him and be a part of the administration of the land. All the demands of different groups were satisfied mutually. Hence, they accepted the offer made by Sukaphaa. He gelled well with the people who were living near the Brahmaputra river and their culture. He made few administrative levels like *Burphagohain* and *Borgohain* for higher rank officers and started ruling the major part of northeast India.

Many rulers succeeded Sukaphaa. Everyone tried to expand their kingdom according to their capacity. The distinct nature of Ahomese kings was they got mixed with their subject's religion, tradition and culture. They did not impose their personal beliefs on anyone. They practised and followed all the traditions of Hinduism. The lore said that the Ahomese kings had lineage from Lord Indra. Hence, the king of Ahom was called *Swargadeo*, i.e., the king of heaven. They built and also reconstructed many temples of various deities; one of them was the re-structuring of Kamakhya temple. Kamakhya temple is one of the most important *Shakti Peeth* in India. For many years, kings, with their subjects, lived a very happy, satisfied and prosperous life in the Brahmaputra belt.

They shared boundaries with Mughals, Manipur kings, Jaintia and Koch kingdoms. The expansionist policy of Akbar disturbed the peaceful establishment of the Ahomese. Akbar wanted to bring all of Hindustan under his reign. Many skirmishes happened between the Mughals and Ahoms. But the major wars that started between the Mughals and Ahoms were during the rule of the cruellest ruler of the Mughals. Aurangzeb aimed to expand his empire as much as he could. He was not at all concerned with ethics, morals or values. Winning the territories and converting the Hindus into Islam were his objectives. The fertile and rich land of Brahmaputra attracted him even more. He started planning to conquer the land in northeast India.

Meanwhile, the kingdom of Koch, which was also called Koch Bihar, was separated into two states due to internal conflicts between the royal brothers. Aurangzeb took advantage of this situation and made friends with one of the brothers. This increased the power of the Mughals.

In the year 1662, the mammoth-sized Mughal army, with the help of the Koch army, marched towards the Ahom Kingdom. The attack was very much fierce and strong. Ahom was not ready for such an attack. They lost the battle. They were asked to give away Guwahati city to Mughals; it was a major city for the Ahom Kingdom.

The king of Ahom, Chakradhar Singha, became really upset due to this severe loss. He had several meetings with all his ministers. Ahom needed someone who could stop the Mughals and also recapture Guwahati for the Ahoms. All of them collectively decided to make Lachit Borphukan their commander-in-chief. He was extremely brave, clever, and a great patriot. He was well-versed in warfare techniques. He was not only strong but also witty. Lachit was the perfect amalgamation of power and intelligence. He was a learned scholar who had knowledge of all the holy scriptures. His faithfulness towards the Ahom Empire was renowned. He was the best pick for the Ahoms to get back their lost pride and defeated territories.

One incident worth noting shows his sincerity towards his work and truthfulness for his nation. When he was appointed the commander-in-chief of the army, he carried out many projects in the territory, which were necessary for fortifying the kingdom. For one such project, Lachit instructed his maternal uncle to finish a certain piece of very important work, which would help in strengthening the borders. He was given some stipulated time. He appointed some soldiers for the same piece of work with his uncle. Everybody started work. One night, when he went to the workplace only to verify the status of the work, he was shocked to see the condition of the work. Everyone including his uncle were fast asleep. Lachit expected the work to be on the verge of completion, but it was far from being accomplished. He was furious at the laziness of his uncle and ordered his fellowmen to behead his uncle.

He said, "Nothing is more precious to me than my country. The laziness of a person could be dangerous for my army and eventually for my nation." This incident spread like fire, and people became aware of his love for the nation, his strictness and dedication towards his work to the extent that he didn't even spare his family.

Now, it was time for Lachit to fight against the mighty Mughals. Aurangzeb sent one of the bravest *sardars*, Raja Ram Singh, son of Raja Jaswant Singh, to destroy the Ahoms. He approached Ahom with a large army. All wars needed a great amount of planning. Lachit played a trick to stop the approaching army and to buy time for preparation. He sent his clever men to negotiate and also to bring an end to the fight in a peaceful manner. Ahoms knew that the Mughals won't be compromising and they will definitely engage in battle. Lachit decided to use guerrilla warfare technique to fight against the Mughals. Guerrilla warfare technique was often used by smaller armies against larger armies. This was the same technique used by the great Maratha king, Shivaji Maharaj.

During the period of 1669–1670, many battles took place between the Mughals and Ahoms. Most of them were won by Ahoms. Lachit's techniques worked well in many regions. But he lost severely in the battle of Alaboi Hill. An unfortunate incident happened where the king of the Ahoms, Chakradhar Singha, died due to a prolonged illness. The Ahomese were in severe grief during that period. The new king, Udayaditya Singha, was enthroned. Many responsibilities burdened Lachit. He was surrounded by many problems. The fresh king was naïve; the Mughal army was waiting on the borders to terminate the Ahom Empire. The Ahomese were in extreme sorrow because of all adversities in the empire. It was a difficult time for Lachit, the commander-in-chief of the Ahom Kingdom. Such despairing situations were the true assessments of real heroes. They must find ways to get out of such situations. Initially, Lachit started making allies with the neighbouring kingdoms. He first joined hands with the Koch Bihar king who was not an ally of the Mughals. He also made peace treaties with the Janitia king and the Manipur king. He made sure they would be of good support during the ensuing war.

Lachit foresaw the wars, and hence, he continued making strategies. He studied the region that would be suitable for his soldiers to fight. He knew the weaknesses of the Mughals. The Mughals ruled only the landlocked areas in India. They didn't have any strong navy. Also, the rivers other than the Brahmaputra didn't have such a big basin for the Mughals to build a strong navy for inland river wars. Hence, the Ahom army started making mud buildings in the open grounds of Assam, so that the battle on land would be very difficult for such a large Mughal army. As Lachit's army was well-versed in fighting a war in the Brahmaputra river, he decided to confront the Mughals in Saraighat. Saraighat was in Guwahati, which was at the border of Ahom's territory. The huge army of Mughals consisting of elephants and horses would find it difficult to move in such areas.

Lachit was fully prepared for the inland naval war. The Brahmaputra river's basin is very huge. The armies should be well-prepared with warships to win the battle of Saraighat. The things were unfolding the way the Ahoms wanted. But all of a sudden, Lachit Borphukan fell sick. The doctors asked him to take complete bed rest. This broke the moral of the Ahom soldiers. Everyone was worried since their leader was on bedrest, and the mighty Mughals were approaching to destroy the Ahoms.

Another ill-fated thing that happened was that Shaistha Khan, Aurangzeb's uncle and Sardar of Bengal joined Ram Singh in the war with his army. The Ahom army had never expected this coming their way. But the real test of any commander is an awful time. Lachit's army started retreating from the war ground. He received the news about this. He stopped his retreating army and said, "If you want to run away from the battlefield, you are free to do that. But I will fight with the Mughals. My king has handed me this responsibility, and I shall fulfil it. Let the enemy abduct me or kill me, but I will fight. You do tell our king that Lachit fought till his last breath and followed the Supreme's orders." Such inspiring words motivated the Ahom army. They got ready for the war again, this time even more charged up than ever.

The Mughals came to know that Lachit was planning for the battle. They knew his calibre. So they tried to make up a fake story about Lachit in the Ahom region to ensure their easy victory. They managed a fake letter to King Udayaditya Singha saying Lachit was paid a sum of one lakh rupees to evacuate the Guwahati war area and that because of him, Ahom lost Guwahati. They also mentioned that he should be fired for such a heinous crime. When this letter reached the king, he initially trusted that letter. His prime minister, Atan Buragohan, convinced the king that it was just a trick to malign Lachit's image. When nothing paid off, the Mughal army prepared for the battle. They had 30,000 infantry, 18,000 Turkish cavalries, 15,000 archers, 5,000 gunners and over 1,000 cannons besides a large flotilla of boats. It was much larger than that of Ahoms' army strength.

Both armies, along with their navies, were ready for confrontation. One of the biggest inland naval wars in the history of India took place. The Ahom army tied their ships together, made a bridge breadthwise on the river, and marched towards the Mughal army. They used all their wits and knowledge of naval war. The magnitude of Brahmaputra was very large in size. The area was very familiar for Ahoms, so they understood every drop and its movement in the river. It was said that Lachit's army tied swords on the back of tortoises, which cut the Mughal soldiers who tried to swim over towards Ahom. Ram Singh's army was destroyed by Ahoms. Many important fighters of the Mughals literally drowned in the Brahmaputra river. Lachit crushed the Mughals to an extent that they started receding from the battlefield. But the Ahoms didn't stop even when they acquired Guwahati back under Swargdeo's reign. They continued their attack till Manas River. Ram Singh and Saishta Khan didn't have any other option but to withdraw their troops. More than 5,000 Mughal soldiers drowned and were killed on the battlefield. This was a major setback for the mighty Aurangzeb. Shivaji in the South and Lachit in the East made Aurangzeb's life miserable. His rampant Islamification of India was stopped by these two warriors. After this war, the downfall of Mughals started, which never stopped.

Lachit showed an amazing piece of leadership and courage on the battlefield. He demonstrated how planning and correct decisions can help your army win combats. His leadership set an example for future generations. He must be remembered for his valour. NDA (National Defence Academy of India), Khadkwasala, Pune, honours the best cadre of the year with the Lachit Borphukan Award. Every army officer is expected to show such kind of bravery on the battlefield.

The User Manuals

"One should perform karma for the benefit of humanity with an unbiased approach because bias gives birth to evil, which creates thousands of obstacles in our path."

— *Rigveda*

"श्रुति स्मृति पुराणोक्त फल प्राप्यर्थं"

This sentence was recited by Rohit a couple of times during the house warming ritual (*Vastu Shanti Pooja*). The pundit asked him to chant this Sanskrit mantra several times during the *Pooja,* and then he offered different things like flowers, fruits, dry fruits, rice, leaves, etc. to the deities. Rohit and his wife, Shweta, followed the given orders by the pundit. Rohit wanted to perform all such rituals with utter devotion, but as he was unaware of the meanings of the Sanskrit *shlokas*, he was really very curious to know about the meaning and importance of the rituals. He didn't have the slightest idea that the answers he was seeking for those queries were going to reform his life forever.

The pooja ended after some time. Everyone feasted on the delicious meal prepared by the ladies in the house. The pundit was loading the pooja stuff in his bag to leave for the day. There were around ten kins who had visited for this auspicious ritual. Rohit asked the pundit if he had some extra time to discuss something as he had some queries regarding the pooja performed. The pundit was affirmative and said, "Yes, tell me! What would you like to know?"

Rohit glanced at Shweta and other family members. They were looking at him. Rohit asked, "We recited many shlokas and *mantras* in the last couple of hours. Could you tell me what they were all about? I would love to know how these shlokas entered the performance of our rituals. Who composed them? How will this help me in life?"

The pundit smiled and said, "Oh! Sir, you have so many questions, and all are genuine ones. I will try to answer you as much as I can. I will apprise you of what I learnt from my Guru.

When we purchase some object, for example, a mobile phone, there is a 4–5 page document for the user to use it effectively. It contains dos and don'ts. This user manual tells you what is good for the mobile's longevity. It also tells us about how much the battery should be charged, what should be kept away from the cellphone for longer and better durability. Such a guide is prepared for a non-living instrument, which we use barely for a maximum of two to three years. But we expect our body to function for more than eighty years. Also, we know that this body is the most sophisticated but complex machine. We need to keep the hardware (body) and the software (mind) going. So we need a 'manual', which can tell you what is good and useful for humans and what is not. It should tell you how you should live your life to the fullest. In our culture, we have such a large collection of scriptures; one cannot read and understand them in a single life. You must have heard of the *Vedas*, *Upanishads*, *Puranas*, etc."

Shweta nodded and said, "Yes we have heard about them. They are ancient books. However, we are not aware of its content. Could you please elaborate about them?"

The pundit continued, "Yes, they are a large collection with many volumes. They contain almost everything about the universe. They contain thousands of verses and many more hymns. Rishi Vyasa compiled them in four *Vedas*. *Veda* literally means knowledge; the knowledge of 'nature of reality'. *Rigveda*, *Yajurveda*, *Samaveda* and *Atharvaveda* are the names of the *Vedas*. Each Veda has particular knowledge. The *Rigveda* has knowledge of science, the matters of the universe like sun, moon, air, body, etc. The *Rigveda* was the first Veda among all. During the period of *Vedas*, that is approximately 12,000 BC, the five elements of nature were worshipped. Idol worship was not practised during that time. Even your name Rohit (name of Sun) came into existence because of the tradition of praying to the Sun God. We worshipped them so that the five elements—*Prithvi* (earth), *Jala* (water), *Tejas* (fire), *Pavan* (air) and *Akash* (void)—that encompasses everything on this planet should bestow their blessings on the human beings."

"With this mine homage I invoke Agni for you, the Son of Strength.

Dear, wisest envoy, skilled in noble sacrifice, immortal, messenger of all."

– Samaveda

"*Yajurveda*, the next Veda created, gives knowledge of all the deeds and duties to be performed by men, women, students, leaders, kings, agriculturists, etc. One should be aware of one's duties. In *Samaveda*, we learn to worship God who gives us peace and long, happy life etc. In this Veda, details of yoga, philosophy, qualities, supreme deeds, and the nature of God are also mentioned. *Samaveda* has songs about God. Almost all *Vedas* tell us about *Karma Kanda*, the rituals one must perform. Today we performed one of them, i.e., the *Vastu Shanti Pooja*. The last but not the least, the Veda that is the most significant one is the *Atharvaveda*. It has details of God, medical science and details of medicine, etc. Here we get the knowledge of Ayurveda which is in use even today. Rohit and Shweta, you both must have heard and recited the Shlokas of *Atharvaveda* in your marriage, though you may not be aware of it."

Rohit and Shweta exchanged a smiled and Rohit said, "This knowledge is amazing and important. One of my friends from South India told me that they have a tradition in which they should pray to one star in the sky during the marriage ceremony. Such rituals must have some meaning to it."

The pundit said, "Yes, it has a very significant meaning. The star you are saying is not one star, but they are actually two. They were called *Arundhati* and *Vasishtha* by our *rishis*. We can only see them as one with our naked eyes. Usually, in space, one star is stationary, and the other revolves around it, but this is not the case with Arundhati and Vasishtha. They revolve around each other; the ideal way a couple should be. It is not the duty of only one person in a relationship to conduct it gracefully, but both should play an important role in conducting the relationship. Our rishis knew about the movement of stars much prior to the invention of the telescope. We have such extensive knowledge in our scriptures."

"Do not be led by others, Awaken your own mind, Amass your own experience, and decide for yourself your own path."

– Atharvaveda

"You have recited this श्रुति स्मृति पुराणोक्त फल प्राप्यर्थ line many times during the pooja performed today wherein you are asking the Almighty to bless the performer of the pooja with whatever benefits are written in the ancient texts like *Shruti*, *Smriti* and the *Puranas*. The *Vedas* are *Shruti* scriptures. It is believed that rishis, in the state of *Tapasya*, heard the *Vedas* directly from Parameshwara, the Almighty. In other words, the rishis attained this knowledge in the state of *Samadhi*, which is called Shruti. So, Vedas are called अपौरुषेय, which means it is not created by any individual, i.e., authorless and believed to be the words of *Ishwara*, the eternal.

Smriti means that which is remembered or which is based upon memory. Smritis are very much relatable to each one of us. In other words, these are produced out

The User Manuals

of human intellect. These are texts that were composed by rishis and handed to our generations by tradition. So, in contrast to Shruti, which is authorless (divine origin), Smriti is produced out of intellect that is usually attributed to an author. Smriti texts were written on the basis of or inspired by Shruti. Major Smriti scriptures are eighteen *Puranas*, *Itihasa*, i.e, *Ramayana*, *Mahabharata* and *Bhagavad Gita*, etc.

The Puranas have many wonderful stories, which have moral values and lessons for life. The rishis have personified the nature of God into different forms for a better understanding of philosophy in scriptures. It has a wide variety of subjects like cultural history, politics, education system, taxation theories, organisation of army, theories on appropriate causes of war, diplomacy, local laws, building public projects, water distribution methods, trees and plants, medicine, *Vastu Shastra* (architecture), gemology, grammar, metrics, poetry, food, martial arts and many more. Even the stories from our great epics, *Ramayana* and *Mahabharata* teach us so much about life. One should understand the stories and learn from them instead of debating about the existence of the characters in the epics."

Shweta interrupted the pundit and asked, "Could you give us one example like how we can learn from our own *Puranas* instead of picking self-help books in today's market?"

The pundit smiled and said, "Today's self-help books contain the same principle which is there in our age-old scriptures only in contemporary language and with modern examples. Examples change with time.

I will recite a story from *Bhagavata Purana* (one of the *Puranas*). It talks about the relationship of a snake and a mouse, which describes how one should be on good terms even with enemies to temporarily solve his problems. It is very much relevant in today's political and even in the corporate world. A snake charmer had locked up a snake in a wooden box. Somehow, a mouse entered into the box in search of food. Upon seeing the snake, which usually preys on the mouse, it got frightened. But the snake told him not to fear, but to bore a hole in the wooden box so that both of them could escape from there. A mouse has the ability and strength in its teeth to bore a hole in the wood. It believed the snake's words and made a hole in the box through which both escaped out. Immediately after coming out of the hole, the snake swallowed the mouse. There are such intriguing stories in the *Puranas*.

There is a scripture you all know about, but it is read only by the older generation, which contains the summary of all *Upanishads, Shrutis, Smritis* and *Puranas*."

Rohit's cousin, Sushant, immediately said, "It is the *Gita*. Am I right? It is a very important scripture, but the only thing I know about it is that it contains dialogue between Arjuna and Lord Krishna. What additional information do we have in the book?"

The pundit nodded and asked for a glass of water. He drank the water, wiped his mouth and said, "Yes, it is a dialogue between two friends. Arjuna had many questions

The User Manuals

regarding the necessity to fight the war with his close relatives, teachers and friends. He was unable to decide what was right and what was wrong. He was unable to take decisions. Such situations often come into our lives. We are Arjuna many times in our lives; sometimes the battlefield is personal, professional or social. Lord Krishna has given solutions to solve all our problems. He tells us the qualities of an imperturbable person. An imperturbable person doesn't get affected by the outcomes. He is stable in happiness and in sorrow. The Lord tells us to do whatever is there in our capacity and not think of anything beyond our control. To give you an example, a batsman can have control over his skills, on his vision at the ball and on his shot selection, but he cannot control the bowler. He has to be ready for any kind of delivery from the bowler. On the same lines, we should also be ready for any situation and not get controlled by our emotions.

We give too much privilege to others. If their activity is favourable for you, you become happy, but if not, you are enraged."

Everybody in the room was listening to the pundit keenly. Everyone goes through such doubts on a daily basis. Sushant asked the pundit with a grin, "What should one do about the sense organs, sir? To give you an example, I know many times that I should avoid eating something, but I am unable to control my desire. Does the Lord have an to answer to this?"

"Yes, our greatest text in the world called *Gita* has every damn answer. The Lord says one should not be a slave of the senses. One should make the senses his or her slaves. The senses are there for functioning according to our orders and not force us to act according to their wish. To give an example, eyes are to see, but it is at our discretion what we should see. Hence, the final decision of what to see, to eat, or to hear are in our hands. Any more queries, my friend?"

Sushant thought for a while and asked, "People worship God a lot and expect so much from him, but all the wishes don't get fulfilled, why is it so?"

The pundit replied, "There is some confusion about God in our culture. Actually, God is just a charioteer of our life as he was for Arjuna. He can only take you to places, but it is you who has to decide where to go. Also, a consistent effort without getting attached to the result is also an important message given by Lord Krishna.

A sensible man is one who thinks beyond himself. Take a simple example; a common man thinks of using plastic as it is very easy to use, but a sensible man will think about the whole ecosystem and find a solution for all the generations. The Lord says that one should always understand that what is noble for the society is helpful for an individual.

The Gita is for everybody; from teenagers to oldies. It is the best user manual one can swear by to lead a successful and happy life. Such is the power of this wonderful text. If we say that this world is a home, then India is the prayer room of this house. Such exceptional knowledge with spiritual experience is a gift to the world from India."

The User Manuals

Rohit looked at his family and turned to the pundit and said, "Thank you so much for this knowledge, sir. Many doubts got clarified today. They were lingering in my mind for years. One last question, sir. All these texts are very useful, but how can we be eligible to get to heaven if it is the highest goal of life?"

The pundit immediately replied, "This is the biggest misunderstanding we all have. Heaven is not the ultimate goal, but *Moksha* or liberation is. Moksha or *Mukti* is a central concept, and the utmost aim is to attain it through different paths during human life. No one up in heaven is operating your life. *Karma*, the most used word in India and the word least understood by us, means you shape your own life. This is a living cosmos. To give an analogy, if you blow a soap bubble, the bubble is real. But if the bubble breaks, only a drop of water falls down. The rest of the bubble will be gone. The air in the bubble will merge with the air around. Mukti means to break the cycle of karma. Why would you want to break the cycle? People think if you are miserable, you will want to break the cycle. Not at all. A miserable person will want to come back richer, better, healthier, taller, more beautiful, more whatever else. Only a person who has seen life in all its facets would want to go beyond this. Hence our motive in life is to attain liberation where we find the utmost happiness. I hope I've made it clear!"

Coast Guards

"Practical patriotism means not a mere sentiment or even emotion of love of the motherland but a passion to serve our fellow-countrymen."

– Swami Vivekananda

Aditya had a habit of showing off a lot. Being the son of a top officer of the Indian Navy, he always received more attention and respect than anybody else in our group. But sometimes such people answer so many questions of ours. The events unfolded accordingly.

There was a seminar arranged in our college on *INS* (Indian Navy Ship) *Vikrant*, the only aircraft carrier that India possessed during the India–Pakistan war in 1971. *INS Vikrant* was a huge asset for India and crucial for national security. That ship was one of the reasons behind our tremendous victory over our neighbouring enemy. I, along with my college group, attended the seminar and in that mood, we went to a coffee shop alongside our college campus, where we ordered different types of coffees. We all sat on one table and started having our coffees.

Aditya took the first sip, and as anticipated, he began to blow his own trumpet. He said, "I visited this *INS Vikrant* ship last year. It was docked in the Mumbai port so that the navy officers and their families could visit it. It is really a massive boat as we all saw in the photos shown in the seminar. I learnt so much about the history of the Indian Navy and also about the current technologies used in warfares." Subodh used to get irritated quickly because of Aditya's over-smart attitude.

Subodh asked, with the intention of humiliating Aditya, "Okay, Aditya! Then can you please tell us something about the history of the Indian Navy? Who was the discoverer of the navy in our country? Our school curriculum educates us only about the present status of Indian armed forces." It was an unexpected question for Aditya.

He thought for a while, took a sip of his coffee and said, "India has a tremendous history of navy. It is one of the major reasons behind being recognised in the world as a Golden Sparrow for a long time in our history. You will be surprised to know that the first tidal dock was built around 2300 BC during the Harrapan civilisation to have smooth trade with Egypt and Mesopotamia (today's Iraq, Kuwait and Syria). Even the *Rigveda*, the oldest Veda, had hymns related to naval and other complementary things of a navy. *Atharva Veda* educated us about the construction of boats and ships. It enlightened us about the correct dimensions of the boat, the material necessary and accurate assembling of the required parts to make a boat. Chandragupta Maurya, the first emperor of India from the Mauryan dynasty, built various ships for safeguarding the empire from outsiders. For more than 1500 years until the 18th-century, foreigners also visited

India to learn the ship-building techniques. For example, the Indian man who helped Vasco da Gama to reach India had thrice as large ships as Vasco da Gama. His ships were towed by the Indian ships to reach Calicut."

After hearing such amazing facts, everyone found interest in knowing more about what was there in India's glorious past. So, Shankar who was from Tamil Nadu, asked Aditya, "As the sea around India is mostly in the southern half of the country, so there might be some possibility that kings from South India also contributed in the development of navy and in different naval excursions?"

Aditya smiled and replied, "You are absolutely right, Shankar. Kings from the South had a large contribution to our navy. They not only safeguarded the coast from aggressors but also initiated trading with the South-Eastern countries. Many ambitious kings who belong to the Chola dynasty played a major role. The years between 985–1042 AD were considered very crucial for the upliftment of India's naval power. Rajaraja Chola and Rajendra Chola I carried out many expeditions to Ceylon, i.e., today's Sri Lanka. Many other countries like Maldives, Sumatra Islands and Indonesia were also explored by the Chola dynasty rulers. They built a good relationship with these countries. This led to a tremendous amount of foreign trade. And we all know that healthier the trade, more are the chances of economic prosperity of the country. Such sensible associations among different countries brought well-being in the subcontinent.

Rajendra Chola built ships, which could carry more than 100 men at a time. The ship-building manufacturing hub was so huge that it constructed 700–1000 ships in a short duration. All types of ships were built. They were for a specific purpose or maybe for multipurpose. Some vessels were for warfare, some were for trade and some for travelling. Every type required different engineering and construction altogether.

India is also a land of scholars, artists and experts. We managed to construct each of the required types very efficiently. Cholas also constructed ships for sailing through rivers as South India had many perennial rivers. They also had a naval force and a naval dock in the coast of the Kaveri river. They had a stronghold in those geographical areas. The dry docks that were constructed by Rajaraja Chola exist even today. Cholas, along with bringing prosperity to the kingdom, also expanded Hinduism in various parts of the world, which showed people a perfect and the easiest way of life. Many countries from South-East Asia follow Hinduism even today. Angkor Wat, the largest Hindu temple, or in fact, one of the largest religious places in the world, is not in India but in Cambodia. There are many idols of Indian Gods found submerged in the sea near Indonesia."

Everyone was listening with keen interest. Another question that I asked him was, "In the Arabian Sea, there are few forts. So there must be some contribution of Maharashtra in the history of Indian Navy as well, hence the explanation for the construction of sea forts?"

Aditya giggled, gave me a pat on my back and said, "Oh! My son of great Shivaji Maharaj, the answer is yes! The Maratha Empire had a long history related to safeguarding the coastal borders of our nation from enemies. I won't be exaggerating if I say that the British could have started ruling us well before 1818 if the Maratha Kings didn't focus on the naval force."

I felt great after hearing this, and my interest increased even more. I kept my coffee mug aside and enquired further, "Could you tell us more about the Maratha's naval power?" and I looked at everybody else and said, "I also wonder sometimes how come the Maratha army sustained after the death of Sambhaji Maharaj and before the rise of the great Bajirao Peshwa? Between the year 1689 to 1720, the Maratha army didn't have any strong leader to guide them."

Aditya again tapped on my shoulders and said, "Actually, one of the major reasons for the survival of the Maratha Kingdom was their strong naval base. Shivaji Maharaj focused on safeguarding the water along with the land. He built 200 strong fighting ships, but the hero of our story is someone else. His name is Kanoji Angre. He was famously called in Marathi as '*Samurdatla Shivaji*' (Shivaji of the seas). He was appointed as the *Darya Saranga* (Admiral) of the Navy in 1698. By the end of the 17th century, the Dutch, the Portuguese and the British were acting in full force to colonise India. They attacked India many times in the 17th and 18th century. Kanoji Angre initially started attacking the merchant ships of British East India Company. These merchant ships had a huge amount of commodities of trade. He looted them and used the finances for the betterment of the Maratha Kingdom.

We have many such incidences related to Angre. He once abducted a merchant vessel from Calicut along with several English sailors and took them to the harbour. He blew up British ships many times found near the coast. He remained a constant threat to the British Navy. British declared him as a pirate and a major threat for the British Empire. Kanoji's valour spread like fire. The British East India Company feared bringing any merchant ships into the Arabian Sea.

Kanoji Angre managed to convince Chhatrapati Shahu and *Peshwa* (Prime Minister) Balaji Vishwanath to increase naval presence even more on the Western coast. With proper planning and with hardworking companions, he managed to create a strong naval base in West India. His navy stood like a wall from any attack. His bravery and commitment were recognised by King Shahu, and he was made the chief of twenty-six forts. Angre created an operating base, somewhat like headquarters, on the islands near Alibaug. He not only won battles but also made sure that any foreigner who tries to do business and exploit Maratha Provinces will be taxed. This improved the economy of the Maratha Kingdom. The tax was called *Chouth*."

"The growth of the Indian Navy was disturbing the expansionist Europeans. They planned to stop this *Darya Sarang*. Charles Boone was appointed as the new

Governor of Bombay province in 1715. He made several attempts to capture Angre and tried his best to win against the Marathas. But Kanoji was not only successful in ensuring the failure of Charles's attempts but also captured the ships of the British and included them in the Maratha navy. Three major war-fighting ships of the British Navy were captured by the Marathas. After this victory, Kanoji intensified the battle even more. His navy attacked the yacht of the British President of Bombay, William Aislabie. In that attack, Marathas killed Thomas Chown, who was the chief of the Karwar factory. Kanoji captured Thomas' wife as a hostage until the British paid him the sum of Rs. 30,000. The East India Company became helpless in front of Maratha's Darya Sarang.

By now, the British General, Robert Cowan, understood that he could not defeat Angre single-handedly. So, Robert Cowan made a pact with the Portugal viceroy, Francisco, to attack the Marathas. They used their best technique called 'men-of-war'. In this men-of-war, the sailors of ships were heavily armed soldiers with advanced ammunition. The British and Portuguese felt that this technique would guarantee victory for them. 6000 men with big ships attacked Maratha's coastal boundaries, but Kanoji was ready with his efficient soldiers. He defeated both the approaching armies and won the battle. This gave tremendous confidence to the Maratha soldiers. Kanoji remained undefeated. He ensured that the Maratha Empire stood strong and confident. He made peace and trade pacts with foreigners like the Portuguese to stop frequent attacks. Vijaydurg Fort was also selected as one of his headquarters. He too prepared men-of-war named '*Pal*' (quick run) and used it in further battles. Kanoji's strength reached such heights that he even kept some Europeans in his army to serve *Swarajya* with him. A Dutchman was given the rank of Commodore to serve the Maratha navy. Angre also tried his hands at the Bay of Bengal. He established a naval base far away on the Andaman Islands.

So my friends, hope your doubts are laid to rest."

All of us were hearing the story with our mouths open. We thanked Aditya for all the insights he gave us about our real heroes. Our coffee mugs were still filled with coffee.

Kannadi Queens

"I can't stand with a person who can betray his own people for the sake of some amount of money." This was a very audacious statement for a woman from the 16th century made to her husband. This dashing lady was Rani Abbakka Mahadevi from the Chowta dynasty. The Chowta dynasty ruled in the area of Moodabidri near Mangalore city in Tulunadu (present-day Karnataka). Coastal Karnataka was guarded by Chowta's kingdom. They had their capital in Ullal (Near Mangalore). Rani was taught about every aspect required in any battle. She learnt sword fighting, horse riding, archery and some different war strategies also. Rani and her two daughters were the pioneer members of the Chowta dynasty who fought against the foreign power. They saved their territory from the greedy invaders during the years 1530–1599. Rani Abbakka was crowned the princess of Ullal.

As Rani grew up, she handled many responsibilities in the kingdom. She built a Shiva temple called Rudra rock. The Ullal region became prosperous as spices, which had lucrative value, were cultivated there on a larger scale. The trade between Chowta and Arabs flourished during this period. Rani made sure that her subjects gained an appropriate price for the commodities. Such wealth attracted many outsiders. So to protect her boundaries, she made alliances and strategic partners with the local eminent groups as she knew that camaraderie should exist between different kingdoms in India to stay protected from the attackers. Hence, to increase the strength of her kingdom, she married the King of Banga, Lakshmappa Arasa II.

Lakshmappa and Rani had different motivations in life. He was an extreme miser and untrustworthy, but Rani Abbakka was fully focused on the welfare of the kingdom though she felt restless in such a crafty atmosphere in Banga. In that duration, the Portuguese turned their attention to Karnataka after conquering some regions of Goa. They asked for forts and fertile lands of the Ullal Kingdom in return for some wealth. This was not at all acceptable for Rani but her husband, Lakshmappa wanted to join hands with the Portuguese. Such behaviour of the king was not acceptable to Rani Mahadevi. Hence, she decided to return from Banga to Ullal to manage her kingdom. This was a bold move for any woman.

Lakshmappa Arasa II became furious and decided to teach Rani a lesson when the favourable time arrived. Abbakka developed Ullal as a major port for trade on the West coast of India. Hence, the province became very prosperous, which attracted the Portuguese, the Dutch, the British and many others. Fearing the big ships and armies of Western power, many small kingdoms went into alliance with these Europeans and agreed with their hegemony. On the other side, Rani Abbakka was rising as a strong opposition for these Western forces. She joined hands with Mogaveers, the fisher community of the West coast. She made pacts with the Zamorin of Calicut and other Muslim leaders of Tulunadu. She was prepared for any unexpected occurrences of events.

The Portuguese attacked Rani Abbakka many times in the years 1525–1570. They used all the possible techniques to defeat Rani. They first attacked the South Kanara coast, which was near Mangalore in 1525 and they also destroyed the Mangalore port. The Portuguese even captured the famous Mangalore Fort, but due to the resistance from Abbakka's army, they could not penetrate further South into Ullal. Some years passed in peace. In the year 1556, Portugal, the overambitious country again started malevolent practices. They demanded a huge amount of taxes and respectful tribute from Rani Abbakka. She didn't pay any heed to such demands. The Portuguese sent a large army with Admiral Dom Álvaro da Silveira to destroy the Chowta Kingdom and capture Rani Abbakka. But the opposite happened. The Admiral was completely destroyed by Rani's army, and he went back empty-handed. This was a major setback for the Portuguese. They didn't stop there but tried other tactics to win against the Rani.

The Portuguese attacked Mangalore again for the third time, but this time, they tried the cruellest ways and burnt down the Mangalore city into ashes. There were genocides by the Portuguese army in Mangalore. They didn't spare even children. They burnt the ships, which were used for trade by the Ullal Kingdom. The temples were also destroyed by the cruel Portuguese. They did all these evil tasks only to upset Rani Mahadevi. They thought that she would agree to their terms after such foul methods, but she kept her patience and waited for the correct opportunity to fight them. History repeated itself in the fourth attack of the Portuguese. This time, they targeted Ullal city, but Rani resisted their attack and saved many people's lives.

In 1568, the Portuguese attacked Ullal with the maximum force possible. Their General, Joao Peixoto, advanced with a large army and massive warships to capture Rani Abbakka. All these years, the Portuguese's wish to conquer the West coast of India was not getting fulfilled. This time, they managed to enter Ullal and also capture the city. The General's army surrounded the royal court of Rani, but she managed to escape from the secret routes and took asylum in a mosque. The Portuguese didn't expect a Hindu queen to enter the mosque. On the same night, she contacted her trustworthy people covertly and gathered 200 strong and brave army men around her. She planned everything in just a couple of hours. She took advantage of the darkness of night and mounted a heavy attack on the non-alert Portuguese army. This attack was unexpected for the General and his army.

Rani used her most dreadful weapon called *Agnivana*, which means arrow of fire. Such arrows burnt the Portuguese soldiers. In this attack, the General, Joao Peixoto, was killed along with eighty other Portuguese soldiers by Rani's army. The Admiral, Mascarenhas, marched towards Rani from another side with extra speed but the result was the same that of Joao Peixoto. As the Portuguese leaders fell, the army lost the courage to fight, and they started fleeing to their ships. Even then, the Rani's army marched towards them and took many soldiers into custody. Rani forced the enemy to even surrender the Mangalore Fort. The Portuguese suffered a big defeat and heavy loss. In 1569, the Portuguese attacked Ullal for the sixth time. But this time, they planned properly. The planner was none other than Rani's husband, Lakshmappa Arasa II.

He was offered a large amount of money for help. He was waiting desperately for an opportunity to destroy Rani Mahadevi's kingdom. He unfolded all the secret corridors and war strategies of Rani Abbakka to the Portuguese. They captured the Mangalore Fort again and attacked Ullal. Knowing the might of the Portuguese and Lakshmappa's togetherness, she asked for the help of the Zamorine of Calicut and the Sultan of Bijapur. The Zamorin of Calicut joined hands with Rani. But this time Lakshmappa's treachery won him the war. Rani was arrested and jailed. The Zamorin of Calicut was killed in the battle. Even in prison, she didn't stop her revolt. Fighting for the motherland doesn't require a place. She died fighting in the prison. Even after her death, her two daughters continued to fight against the Portuguese. Rani remained in the minds of people as 'Veera Rani Abbakka Mahadevi'.

Just 250 kilometres from Ullal and a century later, a woman was born though not being of royal lineage, grabbed the opportunity to rule her land for 25 years.

She was called Rani Chennamma or Keladi Chennamma because the place from where she had come was Keladi in northern Karnataka. The kings who ruled Keladi were called the Nayakas of Keladi. One of them was Somashekara Nayaka who ruled between the years 1664–1672. He was a just and powerful king. He had won many battles during his tenure. One day, he met Chennamma in a social gathering in Keladi. She was extremely beautiful and charming. He could not take his eyes off her. He fell in love with her and pursued to marry her. They got married and hence, Chennamma became Rani Chennamma. She learnt the warfare techniques and also understood the grievances of the subjects. Day by day, she grew as a powerful administrator. As the king was busy with the politics of the nation, people used to approach Rani Chennamma for their concerns and complaints. Rani, too, made the best judge possible. Sometimes, she even went against the decision of the king if she felt there was some discrimination happening with anyone. She was a genuine combination of beauty and brain.

All went well, but one day, a dancer named Kalavathi performed in the royal court. Her performance was so brilliant and mesmerising that it charmed the king to the extent that he gave away a large amount of his wealth to her. He appointed her as the royal dancer of the court. He got so infatuated by her, and he started living with her in her house. He lost all his valour and strength because of his lust towards her. Bharame Mavuta, the foster father of Kalavathi, knew black magic, medicines and hypnotism. He poisoned the king and made him weak. These happenings started impacting the politics of the Keladi kingdom. Rani Chennamma was witnessing the downfall of her husband. She tried her best to stop him, but all her efforts went in vain. She became helpless. But she had to stand for her subjects. She knew that there was only one way to keep harmony in the province—by taking all the responsibilities on her shoulders. She knew that this was not the time to get engaged with bangles but with swords. She faced enemies from inside and also from outside Keladi.

Her father, Siddappa Shetty, helped her wherever required. King Somashekara Nayaka became useless for the kingdom by then. Many ambitious people felt that they had the opportunity to sit on the throne. But Rani Chennamma was a big hurdle for them. Even the chief minister, Thimmanna Nayaka, asked Rani to make Veerabhadra Nayaka the king as he was a puppet in the hands of the chief minister. If she agreed to his terms, he promised to support her in day-to-day affairs. Many such senior officials threatened Rani. Even Bharame Mavuta, who was the reason behind the downfall of the king, was eager to declare himself as the king. Many such people even allied to overthrow the queen. But no one was successful in their attempts. The Sultan of Bijapur found the right time to attack Keladi as there was a lot of instability. He sent a big army under Muzaffar Khan to attack Keladi. But everyone forgot that the common people of Keladi considered Rani Chennamma as their ruler. So, they supported her and joined her army.

Together with Rani, they fought against the Sultan and saved the territory. She needed to find a solid and final solution for all such disruptions. She adopted a boy named Basappa Nayaka and trained him in war tactics, administration and enthroned him as the next king. With the help of Basappa, she restored happiness in the kingdom, which was lost after the fall of her husband, Somashekara. She built religious places for people and *dharmshalas* for saints. She spent most of her money on the welfare of the people.

One bold decision of Rani Chennamma changed the history of the Maratha and Mughal kingdoms. In the year 1689, the younger son of Shivaji Maharaj, Rajaram, asked Rani to let him take refuge in her kingdom while he was fleeing to Tamil Nadu from Maharashtra as the Mughal emperor Aurangzeb's army was marching towards him to crush the Maratha Kingdom after the death of Rajaram's elder brother, Sambhaji. All her ministers were reluctant in helping Rajaram as they feared the Mughal's might. But the queen was of a different opinion. She knew that because of Shivaji Maharaj, Hindustan got a hope of Swarajya (Independent Rule) during the inhuman ruling of Mughals. Because of him, Ram Rajya (where people live happily) was restored in some parts of Bharat. So, she decided to give asylum to Rajaram in Keladi. This made Aurangzeb furious. He sent his army to punish Rani Chennamma and take Rajaram into his custody.

Rani successfully stopped every aggression from the Mughals, and Rajaram also managed to reach his destination safely. Retaliating to the Mughal army was not an ordinary thing. This decision of Keladi Chennamma safeguarded the Maratha king and the Maratha Kingdom. This Maratha Kingdom became the Maratha Empire under Chhatrapati Shahu and Bajirao Peshwa. Mughals just remained puppets in the hands of the Marathas. If she had not taken that wise and brave decision, the Maratha Kingdom would have vanished.

4–5 decades before the Rani of Jhansi's birth, another Rani in the South was born, who fought fearlessly with the mighty British. One can say that she was the first woman to fight against the British for independence. She stood bravely in front of the British Empire to save her land; she was Kittur Rani Chennamma. She was born in north Karnataka in Kakati in Belgaum in 1778. Since birth, she was a very courageous girl. She learnt sword fighting and archery at a very young age. She was trained by her family in all brave activities necessary and raised just like any other man of the family. Rani Chennamma was then married to the king of Kittur, Mallasraja Desai, at the age of fifteen. Hence, she was named Kittur Chennamma. He was a very just king, and he gave equal respect to Rani and made sure that she gets involved in the kingdom's policies. They conceived one son after a few years of marriage. The king passed away some days after his son was born in the year 1816. During that time, the British started harassing the Kittur province. Rani had only one hope that she would train her son and he would teach British a lesson one day. But the Almighty had planned something else. Her son died in the year

1824. She was shattered by this incident. The foe was getting stronger, and on the other side, there was no ruler to save the territory.

The British had already started ruling in almost all regions of India. They made a law that native rulers cannot adopt a child and make him their ruler. They will have to submit to British rule. According to the British, Kittur used to fall in the Bombay province under the Governor. The Commissioner, Mr. Chaplin, assigned Mr. John Thackeray to crush the rule of Rani Kittur Chennamma and get it under the sovereignty of the British queen. John Thackeray attacked Kittur with a large army. Rani Chennamma gathered her army and local countrymen and defended her city. In that fierce battle, the British suffered a big loss. Their chief, John Thackeray, was killed in the hands of Rani Chennamma. This defeat was unbearable for the British. Hence, they sent another larger army and surrounded Kittur. This time, Rani knew that she could not win against such a mighty force. She tried different ways of negotiation, but all were futile. Her army defended the fort for twelve days. But as it is said, the biggest enemy of an Indian is an Indian. This was also very true for Rani. Some traitors in Rani's army mixed cow dung with gun powder, which made the guns of the Kittur army useless against the British. Rani was defeated in that battle and was taken into custody. She died in prison after a few years.

Almost in every century, a lady stood up to fight against the dangers for Karnataka. To date, the names of Rani Abbakka and the Chennammas are taken to motivate the people. All three stood for the country in the absence of their husbands. These empowered women took charge in their hands and fought for the people voluntarily. These queens are the real inspiration for every generation of women in India.

India's Contribution to the World

The lecture got over, and we all were glad that the lunch break had started. Everyone from my college group opened their tiffins. We saw Aditya gushing towards us. He looked ecstatic. He said, "We have a history lecture for the next hour in our auditorium. Some visiting faculty is arriving at our campus to deliver the lecture." There was a mixed reaction in our group. Some got depressed thinking that they have to sit for another monologue. Some were happy that after many days, they were getting a chance to sit in an air-conditioned room. Though I was interested in history, I felt a bit gloomy with the thought of attending the lecture. We didn't have any option but to sit for this guest lecture.

We entered the auditorium and took our seats. The AC was very much satisfying. A full stomach plus cool air made the place conducive for a sound sleep. In a couple of minutes, the speaker arrived on the stage, and he was introduced as Mr. Makarand Deshmukh by our professor. He was an Indian, engineer by profession but historian by nature. He had studied a lot about Indian as well as foreign history. The topic of his lecture was 'Proud to be an Indian'. There were approximately 200 students present for the lecture. After the brief introduction of the lecturer and the topic of the day, our professor requested Mr. Deshmukh to kick-start the lecture. He started the lecture by greeting dignitaries and the audience. The next hour of our lives was full of pleasant surprises. Till then, we didn't know so much about our country's contribution.

Mr. Deshmukh began his lecture with the Harappa and Mohenjo-daro civilisation. These were the oldest civilisations in the world. He apprised the crowd about these age-old cities. He described their creation and maintenance. Our ancestors had built these cities using a foolproof scientific approach. Our forefathers maintained the length-breadth ratio, which was considered a major aspect while constructing cities. These ratios are visible in modern constructions. We got to know about the world-famous universities that were in Bharat like Nalanda and Takshashila. Students from all around the world used to strive to get an education from these universities. The subjects taught there were from every walk of life. Medicines, Mathematics, Astronomy, Philosophy and Spirituality were the different subjects studied by the students in these universities. Every year, 10,000 students used to study in these campuses. Many learned scholars of those times like Chanakya were students of these educational institutes.

He educated us about many great emperors who administered their empire with great humility and ensured the well-being of their subjects. We felt contented to hear that 23% of the world's GDP was from our motherland in the pre-British era. After hearing this, I whispered in my friend's ear, "We took birth in the wrong era." We were listening to him very attentively.

At one point in the lecture, he said something so bizarre that all got shocked and started looking at each other's faces with amused emotions. There was a smell of suspicion in the hall. He stated while narrating the glorious things that even the Pythagoras theorem was from India. He saw that everyone was murmuring among themselves in scepticism. He was expecting such a kind of reply from the spectators. He smiled and stated, "I know this is shocking to you and you are in dubiety right now. But trust me, this is true. Everyone educated you about the theorem and its mathematical usage, but no one informed you about the history behind the theorem."

One boy stood up voluntarily and asked, "Can you please put some light on the history of Pythagoras theorem? What shall be the original name then of the theorem if the inventor is not Pythagoras?"

Dr. Deshmukh replied, "Actually Pythagoras had many learned teachers around the world. He travelled a lot to grasp subjects of his interest. He officially studied in Egypt though he was Greek. Most of his education was done in the central and Eastern parts of Asia, which was the area of Arab countries and India. He reached India and learnt many concepts of Physics and Mathematics from Indian sages. In those days, Baudhayana's *Sutras* were studied for many reasons. *Sutras* have many forms of wisdom. These *Sutras* covered a variety of topics, from Spirituality to Mathematics. Baudhayana's *Sulbasutra*,

India's Contribution to the World

which is also called as Indian *Sulbasutra*, contained many theorems of Mathematics, especially of Geometry. Baudhayana took birth between the ninth and eighth century BC. His correct birthdate is unknown. His teachings were studied across the whole of India. This theorem of the right-angled triangle was one of them.

When Pythagoras travelled to India, he studied and understood the concepts of the geometric triangles. He took the idea from India to Greece. There, he published this theorem by crediting himself. But his contemporary Greeks knew that the theorem was not the original idea of Pythagoras, so they disregarded it. But three-four centuries later, a Roman philosopher named Cicero studied the published theories of Pythagoras and hence, he declared that this theorem was derived by Pythagoras. Euclid, another mathematician, added his understandings to the Pythagorean theories. Many Greek philosophers and mathematicians acknowledged the derived theorem and hence, it spread around the world in the name 'Pythagoras theorem'." We all heard this with our mouths open. We never thought while studying the theorem that its origin was from our own country.

Dr. Deshmukh's next statement bewildered us. He stated, "Let me tell you one more thing. We Indians knew the theory of evolution much earlier than Darwin discovered the theory." Before receiving any questions from the audience, he said, "I will just tell you one theory, and you will support my initial proclamation." He continued, "Everyone knows about *Dashavatar*, the ten incarnations of Lord Vishnu. If you see and understand the chronology of all *avatars* and the forms of every avatar, you will understand it is the same theory that Darwin had conceptualised in his evolution theory.

Let us understand the avatars one by one. The first Avatar was *Matsya* (fish). The initial organism was formed in the oceans, followed by *Kurma*, i.e., the tortoise, an amphibian animal that lives in water as well as on land. The next stage of evolution was terrestrial animals. *Varaha*, the Wild Boar, was the form Vishnu bore in this evolution phase. The boar was followed by *Narasimha*, which is the combination of man and animal, and it is the avatar of the wild and strong beast. He was followed by *Vaman*, the avatar of the dwarf man. We can call him *homo floresiensis* in today's scientific terms or hobbit. Then there was *Parashurama*, the man who lived in the forest without any modern equipment. We can also call him the *Neanderthal*; he was naïve in nature. He was not a fully evolved man yet. He strived on animals and was uncultured. Then, the most sophisticated human evolution took place. Vishnu took the avatar of Lord Rama; well-built, cultured and socially aware. He taught us the right paths to be followed by upcoming generations. This was followed by a full-fledged man, i.e., Lord Krishna who knew everything about the physical and beyond the physical world, i.e., the spiritual world. The ninth incarnation of Lord Vishnu was Lord Buddha, who was the enlightened one. The tenth avatar is yet to appear, and we don't know what surprises we may receive on his arrival on Mother Earth."

The audience seemed to be relating to whatever the speaker was telling. Even I thought that I had been so unaware all this while. We knew everything from our sacred books, but we kept them far away from us as we considered them very colourless and unscientific. We were wrong; there was so much knowledge hidden in these scriptures.

This was one of the best sessions I had attended until now in my life. Dr. Deshmukh was enlightening us about the gospels, which were unheard and lesser-known. He continued surprising us by narrating anecdotes.

He said, "Let me ask you one question. Everybody must have played Snakes and Ladders once in your life?" The audience responded in affirmation. He then said, "Do you have the slightest idea about the invention of the game and the real reason behind the invention?"

One boy stood up and answered notoriously, "Obviously for passing the time. People, then, didn't have privileges like the internet during those days. Hence, for some sort of entertainment, such amusement was required. This game cannot teach you a single thing in life. It is just a game of luck."

The doctor shook his head in disbelief and exclaimed, "My boy! This was exactly not the purpose of the game. This game was invented in India. In this land, the game was called *Moksha Patam*.

Liberation is the highest goal for human beings as per our immortal and eternal *Vedas*. I mean it should be the highest goal, but people have forgotten this now. *Moksha* means the highest liberation. To attain this goal, one should be moral and honest all through their life. While playing this game, ladders were marked for virtuous points and snakes denoted awful points. So, to reach the ultimate goal, one should follow virtuous points. This was the teaching from this simple snake and ladder game. This game teaches you about good and bad karma. The game had references in the old Vedic texts, but actually, Saint Dnyaneshwar from Maharashtra brought this game into the limelight. When the British came to India, they loved this game and took it to their homeland. From England, it went to the USA and became the game of Snakes and Ladders and remained just a recreational activity for kids." By now, such eye-openers were usual for the audience.

Dr. Deshmukh said, "I have covered history by touching mathematics, science and also the game in it. Let me touch the last topic, which is medicine, and conclude the sermon. Do you all know a physician named Sushruta?"

I stood up and answered, "Yes, I read on the internet that he is the father of surgery and Russians have a big statue of him outside their famous medical colleges."

Dr. Deshmukh then said, "Yes, nowadays, the only source of knowledge is the internet. Anyway, you are right! He is the father of surgery and the greatest surgeon of all time. He was from India and not from Russia. He invented plastic surgery around 2,500 years ago. However, people from the West received the Noble Prize for sharing the knowledge of plastic surgery with the world.

This surgery was done in India, especially for the wounded soldiers. So the soldiers could join the army

India's Contribution to the World

again and save the country from the enemy. Sushruta healed their wounds with this knowledge of medical science. For example, if someone wanted to heal a wounded nose, Sushruta used to replace the wounded nose's skin with the extra skin on the forehead or from another part of the body. He had remedies for more than a thousand diseases. *Sushruta Sanhita* was his famous volume on medicine and surgery. Even today, irrespective of the 'pathy' practised by the doctors, *Sushruta Sanhita* is taught in many medical colleges. We have many such discoveries in our ancient India. On this note, I take your leave. Thank you for all your support as a peaceful audience."

We left the auditorium in utter silence. Everyone for sure was thinking in their mind about the last hour of roller coaster ride like a lecture. I was wonderstruck with the information I received about my country's contribution to all walks of life. We helped the world not just in spirituality but also in making day-to-day life easier. That day, I came to know of the real meaning behind the statement made by the greatest scientist, Albert Einstein, that, "We owe a lot to the Indians, who taught us how to count and many other things, without which no worthwhile scientific discovery could have been made."

Avatars of Shakti

Karolina Goswami, a Polish woman who loved India and studied India thoroughly once defined women empowerment in her own words. Empowerment means self-realisation of unique strengths and being confident in who you are. Copying men or making the same mistake that men make is not empowerment. Doing what men do is not empowerment. By copying men, women are restricting themselves, and where there is a restriction, there is no real empowerment. In every field, women are capable of performing, but women must remember competing with men is not in itself empowerment.

In India, women have played an equal part in initiating and maintaining the great heritage and culture. The woman is a strong force in an Indian family. India has produced efficient queens who were great leaders. They participated in every aspect from battles to household work, from managing the kingdom to making the strategies for the nation. As this is the land where *Ardhanarishwara* is worshipped, it is needless to say that equality is in the basics of Bharat. In our history, one can find that in every part of our country, there are many examples where there was strong leadership under a woman. This is a saga of two women who lived the most disastrous personal lives, but the self-realisation of their uniqueness made them admirable.

Malhar Rao Holkar, a trustful commander of Peshwa, served Maratha for a long period. He was called the Lord of Malwa (which is a part of today's Madhya Pradesh) territory. Bajirao Peshwa was very much impressed with Malhar Rao after he accompanied him in the battle of Delhi. One day, Malhar Rao was marching towards Pune. To take rest for a while, he stopped in Chaundi village in Ahmednagar province. Malhar Rao and his army finished the lunch and were about to resume their journey when they heard a loud shout. Everybody looked towards the place from where the voice came. To their surprise, it was the voice of a young girl aged approximately seven-eight years old. Malhar Rao went to that girl, sat on his knees and asked, "What happened, my child? Why are you shouting?"

The girl replied, "You and your army don't have simple manners. See how much food you have wasted. You soldiers know how to ride a horse but do not know how to eat." She pointed at the leftover food in soiled plates. Many plates had a small number of morsels left. She continued, "Many of my friends have nothing to eat for days and you people are wasting so much of God-gifted food. I will complain about this to Raja Shahu."

Malhar Rao was pleasantly struck by the words of that girl. He was extremely impressed with the courage shown by the girl and was amazed to see the concerns for the people she had at such a young age. He held the hand of the girl lovingly and said, "Rani, we all apologise to you. This will never happen again. What is your name, Rani?"

The girl replied, "Ahilya."

Malhar Rao felt that Ahilya would suit in the house of brave Holkars. Hence he met Ahilya's father and requested him to marry Ahilya to his son, Khanderao Holkar. Ahilya's father, who was the chief of that village, immediately agreed as he felt him to be a good match for his daughter. Hence, Ahilya got married to Khanderrao Holkar in 1733 and went to Indore after the wedding as a newly-wed bride. Malhar Rao trained Ahilya and Khanderrao in all areas. He kept a watch on her progress. She learnt warfare techniques and also studied finance. She read different Indian scriptures. Malhar Rao didn't know that he was making a great queen for the future.

After a few years of her marriage, an unfortunate incident happened. Khanderrao was killed on the battlefield by a cannonball. She became a widow at a very early age. Malhar Rao helped Ahilya in coping with the sorrow by involving her more in the administration of the province of Indore. There are many incidents where Malharrao asked Ahilya to go for expeditions, also to take care of the military affairs happening around Indore. One of the most dreadful battles of Panipat took place in 1761. The Maratha army was defeated because of weak planning. Because of Ahilya's administration, Malwa territory was less affected by the consequences of the war.

Maratha's reign started declining after the war. Malhar Rao Holkar died in 1766. This was not it. Ahilya's son, Malerao Holkar, passed away in a couple of months after his father's demise. Ahilyabai was in an awful situation. She had no one to bless her and look up to. There was no one left in the family to rely on. All the family support was gone. But she didn't lose her confidence. As she knew the kingdom of Malwa was becoming weaker and there were many enemies to fight with, she requested Peshwa to let her take over the administration of Malwa province. Peshwa agreed to her terms. She handed the military matters to Tukojirao Holkar, the stepbrother of Khanderrao Holkar. Ahilyabai faced opposition from many minsters, but she crushed that revolt and ruled the province most efficiently.

Those were the times of monarchy. A glimpse of the king or the queen was a rare sight. Reaching the royal court for problems was out of the question for any civilian of the kingdom. Ahilyabai was an exception in this. She was easily accessible and was always available for public hearings. She made sure that there will be justice in her province. She looked into every matter. She sacked the officials who used to take bribes from people to complete their work. All the malpractices that could dysfunction the kingdom like corruption and extortion were stopped by the queen. She was not just the queen but was like a mother to her subjects. She was addressed as *'Matoshri'* (mother) by everyone. She not only solved the problems of her subjects but also found ways to make their lives better. When she started ruling Indore, it was just a small village, but under her reign, it grew as one of the most beautiful and prosperous cities. She was one of the very few rulers that never took taxes from her merchants, farmers and cultivators. She established a textile industry in Indore to give a boost to the economy of people. She made sure that her countrymen would prosper.

Ahilyabai protected the Malwa boundaries from every possible attack from the outsiders. Sometimes, she participated in battles. She even taught a proper lesson to dacoits, who came to rob the houses in the Malwa region. She was threatened by the Mughals, British and many others at different times so that they could win over the provinces under Ahilya. But they never won against her. Ahilya used to have a proper understanding of the enemy. She even suggested the Peshwa regarding the strategy they should have followed while dealing with the British and other foreign attacks. She had described the British in impeccable words. She used to say that other enemies were like the tiger, one that comes to kill you directly, but these British were like a bear. They come to give you a bear-hug. They tickle you and then kill you. Defeating such enemies is more difficult. She had understood that the British had the policy of divide and rule.

Ahilya was not just a brave, confident woman, but she was also emotional and spiritual at heart. She had immense faith in Lord Shiva. She was one of the most important personalities of Indian history who tried to rejuvenate the Hindu sculptures and places in the nation. She built temples across India. Kashi, Gaya, Somnath, Ayodhya, Mathura, Haridwar, Kanchi, Avanti, Dwarka,

Badrinarayan, Rameshwar and Jaganathpuri are the major places where she built temples. She crossed her territory's boundaries and built many temples. She reconstructed many such religious places, which were destroyed by inhuman Islamic invaders. She helped the sages and saints to conduct the Hindu rituals quietly. Though being rich and prosperous, she used all her wealth for the welfare of her subjects. She spent a very humble and selfless personal life. Though she was from a royal family, she didn't stay at the big mansions of Indore, but she spent her life in a pilgrimage place called Maheshwar near the banks of river Narmada. She didn't get attracted to the illusions of life and walked the path like that of a mystic who lived for the betterment of the people. Despite being tortured by her destiny, she changed the fate of countless people. This story showed her love for her kingdom.

A century earlier, another empowered Maratha woman exhibited her strength in adverse conditions.

Maharani Yesubai was the daughter-in-law of the great Maratha king, Shivaji Maharaj. She married his son, Sambhaji Maharaj, at a very young age. Sambhaji and Yesubai learnt many good values, ethics and leadership skills under Shivaji Maharaj. Shivaji made sure that Yesubai, too, participated in the regular activities of Swarajya. He knew that a woman could create tremendous positive changes in society; his mother Jijabai was a great example who imbibed patriotic values in Shivaji. Even the idea of Swarajya was put in his mind by his mother, Jijabai. Sambhaji and Yesubai grew together while getting involved in political matters, and they became very important pillars of Swarajya. Yesubai's love for Swarajya grew day by day. Yesubai was so involved in the Swarajya fabrication that she even went against her brother who demanded Jahangir (province to self-rule) unjustly. She made sure that Sambhaji didn't get disturbed while looking after the Swarajya's boundaries.

There were many challenges that Sambhaji faced in his life. He was even defamed as a traitor by his people. His stepmother, Soyrabai, tried everything to trouble Sambhaji for her benefits. Under a political and strategic move, Sambhaji went and met the enemy and stayed in an enemy camp for a year. This led to a massive upsurge of misgivings among people against Sambhaji. He didn't even inform Yesubai about his political plans. Everyone in Swarajya felt that Sambhaji backstabbed his father. Even his own family went against him. All this negativity was faced by Yesubai on behalf of Sambhaji. People taunted her and demeaned her in all possible ways. But she faced all this with great courage. She was sure that her husband won't betray Swarajya. Their bonding was so strong that any rumour that reached her didn't hamper the trust. She appointed an efficient spy team who could send and receive the messages of Sambhaji Maharaj. In that period of the year, she went through many traumatic situations. But her trust in her husband and on Swarajya was so strong that she overcame all the fears. Sambhaji returned to Swarajya after a year, and she proved to the world that her husband was not a traitor but a patriot.

After the demise of Shivaji Maharaj, it was expected that Sambhaji would take his throne rightfully. When it

Avatars of Shakti

was so obvious that the elder son should be enthroned, Sambhaji and Yesubai had to fight with the internal politics to gain their rights. Sambhaji ruled for nine years before he was caught by Aurangzeb. Yeusbai, with their son, was also taken into custody. Sambhaji was tortured to an extreme extent. He was killed in the prison as he didn't agree to the terms of the Mughal emperor; one of them had to convert to Islam. Yesubai was kept in captivity even after the death of her husband. She still managed to work for Swarajya, keeping the mission of her husband in mind. Though being the daughter-in-law of the greatest Maratha warrior, Shivaji Maharaj, Yesubai spent a very low account life and faced countless difficulties in terms of finance, health and in the family itself. Sita was in Ravan's custody for only one year, but Yesubai was in the Mughals' captivity for more than fifteen years. One can imagine the level of torture she must have faced.

Ahilyabai and Yesubai didn't get anything even after getting married in the most respected families. Only self-realised empowered women can lead such lives ideally. Such personalities are the real inspiration for every generation in India.

Land of Saints

"If you think you are big, you become small. If you know you are nothing, you become unlimited. That's the beauty of being a human being."

– Sadhguru Jaggi Vasudev

India is the only country that promotes '*Vasudhaiva Kutumbakam*', which means this whole world is one family. This world is one home. To make such an inclusive and extremely high-minded statement, a country must have a generous mindset. Such a mindset can only be possible when the culture of the land is humanistic and broad-minded. This country is blessed with many saints and sages who preached this liberal thinking to society. They made sure that the *Vedas*, which we may call as spiritual laws, were passed on generations to generations. These *Vedas* talk about humanity and tolerance.

These saints selflessly spent their whole life for the betterment of mankind. They made the ancient texts understandable for the generations by writing the commentary in colloquial languages of India. Their contribution helped to sustain *Hindu Santana Dharma* in the Indian subcontinent though it was endangered from different invaders who came in as aggressors or as missionaries to preach some foreign religions. It is said

Land of Saints

that in *Kaliyuga*, the evil could be destroyed by knowledge and debates if necessary than wars unlike the *Treta Yuga* and *Dvapara Yuga*—when the criminal was killed, the problem was solved. In Kaliyuga, ideological differences were specifically dominant in nature; not all differences could be solved by war. To deal with such unrighteousness, saints, from time to time, helped India and also the world.

This was the time when Hinduism was divided into many sects. Eighth century AD saw a massive rise in superstitions among people and people had become too ritualistic. They were becoming not God-loving but God-fearing. They had forgotten their karma or duties and engaged themselves in rituals. *Shaivism, Vaishnavism, Smartism, Shaktism* and many such sects were some in which *Hindu Sanatana* (ancient) *Dharma* was divided. The division rose to seventy-two different cults in the eighth century.

On the other hand, Buddhism was emerging largely at that time, and people were voluntarily getting converted to Buddhism to spend a monastic life. People were getting inclined to Buddhism, as it was easier to follow. Even Buddhism involved performing numerous rituals, and the main crux was missing in both Hinduism and Buddhism. In such conditions, a sage rose and in a short span of life, of a mere 32 years, managed to bring back the sanctity of Hinduism and joined all the sects under one umbrella of Sanatana Dharma. His name is Adi Shankaracharya, who tried to bring clarity among people regarding their religion. Being considered an incarnation of Lord Shankar, he was named accordingly. He was born in a small village named Kaladi in Kerala. When he was just three years old, he was well-versed with all the *Vedas*, *Upanishads*, and *Puranas*. He had a strong inclination to ascetic life since his childhood. At a very tender age, he decided to take *Sannyasa* (total renunciation from the material world or detachment from physical entities). He somehow managed to convince his mother to grant him permission for this and left home in search of a Guru who could guide him towards his spiritual goal. He travelled across India in search of a perfect guide for him and reached Badrinath in the present-day Uttarakhand where he finally met his Guru, Swami Govindapada Acharya. Every Guru conducts an exam before accepting the student as his disciple. Similarly, Swami Govindapada Acharya took the test of Shankaracharya and needless to say, he passed with flying colours. Swami Govindapada taught him the philosophies of Hinduism; one of them was *Advaita* philosophy.

Being cognisant with the calibre of Shankaracharya, Swami Govindapada asked Shankaracharya that he should not stay in the ashram and be a hermit like everyone else, but he should go out and serve the people by clearing their doubts about Hinduism. It would be his duty to bring discursive people back to the real teachings of this Hindu Sanatana Dharma. Shankaracharya immediately started his journey with the same purpose. From that day, his philosophical conquest began. He met the leaders of different schools of thought. He met people who had gained authority in particular sects and considered their sects superior to that of others. He convinced them by arguing and established the supremacy and truth of Hinduism. He told them how we all are one and children of the Almighty. He went to all the renowned places for learning. He challenged the learned men for discussion, argued with them and impressed them with his opinions and views. There were two ways to do that—*Khandan*, which means by telling how the understanding of the opponent was wrong and the other was by convincing how Shankaracharya's Vedic understanding is more correct, logical and true, i.e., *Mandan*.

There were Rishis and Rishikas who also challenged Shankaracharya. Dandi and Mayura were taught the correct philosophy as told in *Vedanta*. He then won the heart of Harsha who authored great texts like *Khandana Khanda Kadya*, *Abhinavagupta*, *Murari Misra* and *Udayanacharya*. He faced many troubles during such intellectual fights. Many times, the debates used to last for months, but Shankaracharya always returned victoriously. He had a thorough understanding of the philosophy of Sanatana Dharma. His concepts were crystal clear. Some opponents used to get awestruck and so fascinated by Shankaracharya's answers that they requested Shankaracharya to make them his disciple. With this, he managed to make many disciples and joined people in his journey of spreading the real crux of Hinduism.

He travelled across the whole country many times. He observed that a major chunk of people did not have enough understanding of *Vedas* and *Upanishads*. Hence, he wrote different commentaries on the same. He also wrote interpretations of *Bhagavad Gita* so that a simple layman could understand what Lord Krishna meant. Such commentaries and interpretations explained to people the different ways to pray to the Almighty. The *Bhakti* Movement was prevalent at that time. Shankaracharya integrated the meaning of *Vedas* with the roots of the Bhakti Movement.

During this dedicated work, he made sure that the teachings wouldn't fade away with time. He set up four monasteries (*Mathas*) in four corners of India. The four *Mathas* were at Dwaraka in the West, Jagannatha Puri in the East, Sringeri in the South and Joshimath in the North. Each Math was headed by one of his four main disciples, who carried forward Vedanta philosophies to the other followers of subsequent generations. He also set up a Matha in Kanchipuram. These Mathas also signify the spiritual boundaries of the country as all the four Mathas are located in four different directions of India. He set few rules for future generations, which made sure that the Bharatvarsha remained intact. For example, the Pundit in Rameshwaram temple (situated in Tamil Nadu) must be a Maharashtrian Brahmin and Pundit of Badrinath in the Himalayas should be a Keralite *Nambudiri* Brahmin. There are few more such examples set by Adi Shankaracharya, which made sure the nation remained intact. He was called as *Jagadguru* (teacher of the world) Shankaracharya for his guidance to human beings of the world at large. His guidelines still hold relevance even today.

India faced newer cultural challenges many times. It was at its worst when the British came to rule this land. The plan of Lord Macaulay, the politician in the British Parliament, was to break the backbone of India, i.e., her spiritual and her cultural heritage by replacing the Indian

Land of Saints

education syllabus and teaching Indians the Western philosophies. He intended to dominate the nation by making people lose their self-esteem and become slaves of Westerners physically and especially mentally. He wanted Indians to believe that British rule on them was God's gift for them so that England could exploit India as much as possible. British marketed India in the world in such a way that the whole world started believing that India needed missionaries from outside for their upliftment.

To fight this false propaganda, one Swami stood strong and fought against the missionaries who were turning the plan of Lord Macaulay into action. He is Swami Vivekananda. He preached Vedanta and the importance of Yoga to India and the world. He strongly felt that the time had come to preach to the world the priceless truths contained in Vedanta. When Indians were looked down as uncivilised and as uneducated people by the West, Swamiji stood up high and told the world how fortunate he feels to be born in India and the Hindu religion. It was crucial to acquaint the world with the quality of knowledge this country had.

Swami Vivekananda travelled throughout the country and met people of different opinions and conveyed the message of Vedanta. He tried to give the message to the youth, which would inspire them to stand on their feet and also work for fellow citizens. He boldly commented, "You will be nearer to heaven through football than through the study of the *Gita*. You will understand the *Gita* better with your biceps, your muscles, a little stronger."

"Arise, Awake and Stop not till the goal is reached," was his strong message.

He became famous after his preachings in India. He was called to different countries to deliver the sermons on Vedanta. The more he saw the way propagandists were damaging Indian culture, the more he was convinced that it was in Vedanta that humanity could be assured of a civilised future. Swami Vivekananda became world-famous when he delivered the most historic speech wherein he introduced Hinduism at the Parliament of the World's Religions in Chicago in 1893. He told the world about the inclusive and open-minded nature of Hinduism.

He said in his speech, "I am proud to belong to a religion which has taught the world both tolerance and universal acceptance." He also conveyed the message of Hindu Rishis that the best method of worship would be worshipping God unselfishly. The Vedic Rishis do not call the earthborn as a 'sinner' at all but as children of Almighty or immortal bliss. He mentioned that we all are one and potentially divine souls.

A day after the speech, the newspaper *New York Times*' headline read, "Vivekananda is undoubtedly the greatest figure in the Parliament of religions. After hearing him, we feel how foolish it is to send missionaries to this learned nation." In this way, Swamiji taught not only India but also the world the real spiritual knowledge.

Every generation had saints, monks and spiritual beings to help mankind and to enrich mankind to a higher level. India has witnessed this phenomenon of such a transformation from time to time. But particularly, Maharashtra saw many such saints who blessed this land enormously. Saint Dnyaneshwar, at the age of 16, wrote a commentary on *Gita* in colloquial Marathi, which helped the people to understand the knowledge described in *Gita*. Saint Ramdas Swami wrote many books, which had a wide range of topics. The topics contained knowledge from our basic daily habits to knowledge from the Vedas. He guided people in almost all areas in which an individual faces problems. He had also composed *shlokas* addressing the mind, which are no less than a self-help book. He was the Guru of the greatest Maratha king, Shivaji Maharaj. He asked the people not to work for selfish needs but to join Shivaji Maharaj's army and help him attain *Hindavi Swarajya* (independent kingdom of Hindus). Like Vivekananda, he too asked people to focus on fitness with spiritual understandings.

There were sages in the past who brought so much happiness in the lives of Indians by showing them the correct path. Sages like Gajanan Maharaj and Sai Baba aided people to overcome sorrow and fear in their daily routine. People of this country were blessed by some or the other divine beings that showed them truthful and virtuous paths. Even today, we have mystics like Sadhguru Jaggi Vasudev, Sri Sri Ravishankar and Swami Ramdev, who are showing the world the best way to lead life. They just don't confine themselves to the country, but they spread the message of our culture in every part of the world. They are following the ancient *Vasudhaiva Kutumbakam* theory and are working for the betterment of the world.

The Largest Surrender

"You received three at this age; when I was of your age, I received nine bullets and look today, I am the Commander in Chief of the Indian Army."

– Sam Manekshaw to an injured soldier during the 1971 war

"Subha ka nashta Jaisalmer mai karenge, duper ka khana Jodhpur mai aur raat ka khana Delhi mai."

– (We shall have our breakfast at Jaisalmer, lunch at Jodhpur and dinner in Delhi.)

This was the plan made by Lt. Gen. AAK Niazi of Pakistan on December 2, 1971. Pakistan was all set for another war against India.

It all started in the year 1969 when President Ayub Khan took the first general election in a democratic path in Pakistan. The contest was between Pakistan People Party (PPP) and Awami League. Awami League was headed by Sheikh Mujibur Rehman. Awami League won with an absolute majority in the election. These results were not acceptable to West Pakistan, which was dominated by Punjabis in Pakistan. Awami League initiated the independence struggle against them. This was the party that supported the liberation of Bangladesh from Pakistan.

Bangladesh was East Pakistan before the liberation. Innumerable riots were happening in Pakistan in the year 1969. Bengalis and other ethnic groups were tortured and raped by the Pakistani army and its collaborators. These Bengali ethnic groups formed *Mukti Bahini*, the armed group for their self-defence. But the strength of Mukti Bahini was not comparable to the Pakistan Army. Many Bengali civilians started infiltrating India to take refuge for the living. India, too, helped them initially by setting up various relief camps for them. The Indian states adjoining Bangladesh like West Bengal, Assam, Tripura set the camps along the Bangladesh border. The number of refugees increased tremendously in 1970. The number recorded was ten million. India was trying to succour Bangladeshis. This was a major strain on India's developing economy. The Indian government increased the tax on its citizens to help these migrating Bangladeshis. So, it was an increasing burden on Indians. India was not a strong economy in 1971. India herself was on crutches. Prime Minister Indira Gandhi appealed to the international community for assistance. But no one responded positively. Indira Gandhi supported the independence of the people of East Pakistan and concluded that instead of giving asylum to lakhs of refugees, the only option left was that of a war. Sometimes, to attain peace, war is the only way out.

There was another turn of events, and India got another reason to go to war. On January 30, 1971, an Indian airline plane flying from Srinagar to Jammu was hijacked by Kashmiri separatists who were funded by

The Largest Surrender

Pakistan. They took the plane to Lahore and set it on fire. This enraged people and the government of India. Mrs. Gandhi banned the flying of any kind of Pakistani aircraft over Indian territory.

Even in Pakistan, there were campaigns like 'Crush India' taking place as India was supporting the Anti-Pakistani elements. So both the countries had enough reasons to go to war. On April 28, 1971, Mrs. Gandhi had a meeting with the Chief of the Army, General Sam Manekshaw. In this meeting, she informed him that now the war was inevitable. So she asked, "What is the perfect duration for India to engage in the war?"

General Manekshaw replied, "It would be great if you give me six months for preparation. Beginning the war in winter will be favourable for us. It would be difficult for the Indian Army to get into a war in Bangladesh in the monsoon season. The lands turn marshy during that period because of heavy rain in and around the Brahmaputra basin. And also, if Pakistan asks for China's support, it will be difficult for China to cross the Himalayas in the biting cold winter season. So in six months, we can be in a sure-shot win situation."

Prime Minister Indira Gandhi agreed with General Manekshaw's views and asked him to prepare for the war and also train Mukti Bahini groups to fight with the Indian Army against Pakistan. Those six-seven months were very crucial for India. Mrs. Gandhi travelled across the globe and made strategic alliances with different nations. She tried her best to make sure no country would fight with or support Pakistan against India when the war broke out. She made no war pacts and peace pacts with major forces of the world. India was all set for war by the end of November. India was just waiting for some opportunity to initiate war.

On December 3, 1971, PAF (Pakistan Air Force) launched a surprise strike on eleven airfields of northern and Western India. They reached till Agra airfields, which was approximately 300 kilometres from the Pakistan border. This was the official declaration of war by Pakistan. In response, Mrs. Gandhi too launched a war declaring a national emergency and ordered the mobilisation of troops. All the three forces—army, navy and air force—were just waiting for the orders from top officials. The major aims were to capture Dhaka from Pakistan's Army and also to save our land from West Pakistan.

The war had officially begun in full force from December 3, 1971. The first major strike by the Indian Navy was on December 4th. The Indian Navy attacked the Karachi port with full force. It was a planned move by India. The fighter planes of Pakistan used to get fuel from the Karachi port. Hence the destruction of that port would be a major setback for Pakistan. Pakistan was overconfident that India didn't have enough powerful ships, which could navigate to Karachi from Mumbai port and return to the base location. But India intelligently towed the ships from Mumbai to Dwarka (Dwarka is geographically very close to Karachi) and then went to attack Karachi. This Karachi attack sank many major Pakistani ships including destroyer PNS (Pakistan Navy

The Largest Surrender

Ship) *Khaibar*, minesweeper PNS *Muhafiz*, and PNS *Shah Jahan*. Around 800 Pakistani sailors were killed in this initial strike. Pakistan lost a large amount of reserve fuel due to this attack.

To avenge this loss, Pakistan submarine attacked INS *Khukri* and killed 190 plus Indian soldiers. This boosted Pakistan's confidence, and because of this victory, Pakistan involved more submarines in the war. India didn't waste time and attacked the Karachi port for the second time. This time, it was bigger than before. The Indian Navy sunk many Pakistanis and other foreign ships stationed on the port. The destruction included warships as well as merchant ships. The attack destroyed the fuel reserve even further. This was all happening in the West part of the war, but in the East, India had INS Vikrant, the lone aircraft carrier in the war. India deployed INS Vikrant in the Bay of Bengal, which prevented any help to the Eastern navy of Pakistan. INS Vikrant's Sea Hawk planes attacked many parts of East Pakistan like Chittagong, Cox Bazar, etc. INS Vikrant played a major role in the war hence, Pakistan decided to sink the aircraft carrier. They deployed PNS Ghazi to sink INS Vikrant. But Indian submarines intelligently found the location of PNS Ghazi and sank it in the ocean. Pakistan almost lost half of its navy power in this war. They lost the war in the sea. Around 1,900 Pakistani personnel lost their lives while 1,413 servicemen were captured by Indian forces in Dhaka. PNS then withdrew itself from any conflicts with the Indian Navy.

Indian Air Force played a crucial role in the Longewala War in Rajasthan. The Pakistan Army started infiltrating from the West in Rajasthan. 2,000 infantry and forty-five war tanks crossed the Indian border and started marching towards Longewala post at 12.30 a.m. on December 5th. Under the leadership of Major Kuldeep Singh Chandpuri, 120 courageous Indian soldiers and a Jeep-mounted M40 rifle were safeguarding the post. The armies clashed head-on. The Indian airbase near Longewala was equipped with four Hawker hunters and HAL Marut fighter planes, which were incapable of fighting in the dark. It was a huge responsibility on those 120 soldiers that they had to safeguard the post for more than five hours. They fearlessly managed to defend the post. With the first ray of sun, the Hawker Hunters and Marut immediately took off and destroyed the tanks of the Pakistani Army. The Pakistan Army fled back towards the border, which was initially planning to reach Delhi by the end of the day. This was a memorable incidence in the history of India for Indians, where the combined efforts of the army and air force led to a big victory over the enemy.

One of the most successful air raids by India into West Pakistan happened on December 8, 1971, when Indian Hunter aircraft from the Pathankot-based Squadron 20, attacked the Pakistani base in Murid and destroyed five F-86 aircrafts on the ground. In the East, Squadron 14 Tail Choppers under Squadron Leader PQ Mehdi, which was taken as the Prisoner of War, was destroyed. This resulted in the superiority of Indian air in the East.

The Largest Surrender

As Mrs. Gandhi banned flying of Pakistani flights on Indian air space, Pakistan had to take a long route from the Indian Ocean to send help to East Pakistan. Jordan, Iran, Saudi Arabia and many such Arab countries tried to help PAF, but they couldn't stand in front of the Indian Air Force. Pakistan lost more than seventy-five aircrafts in this war.

In the East, the Indian Army and the Mukti Bahini group were one team in this war against the Pakistan Army. Pakistan thought that they could win the Indian provinces of the West while the Indian Army was busy on the Eastern side of the country. But they were wrong in their thinking. Things went in India's favour. The Indian Army penetrated various regions of Pakistan. They won many areas in Azad Kashmir, Sindh and Punjab. On the Eastern side, the army aimed to conquer Dhaka. Here, the Indian Army used the 'Blitzkrieg' technique, i.e., a sudden attack on the enemy. This full-throttle attack weakened the Pakistan Army. The Indian Army was infiltrating into East Pakistan from all sides. Lieutenant General Jagjit Singh Aurora who headed the Eastern command of the Indian Army asked the Pakistan General, Niazi, to surrender. But General Niazi continued the war, and the destruction in war persisted.

Meanwhile, Pakistan asked for help from the United States of America in the war. The US tried to build diplomatic pressure on India in the United Nations to stop the war. But Russia stood by India's side and played its veto card, and the war continued. Understanding that India would not end the war, the US government asked China to help Pakistan. But due to the freezing December climate, they were unable to send any concrete help to East Pakistan. All the plans made by Indian Army generals showed positive results in due course of the battle. The US then sent its big warship to help Pakistan against India. Then Russia too sent a warship to help India. The war was now escalating. India wanted to finish the war as it may lose the hold on the war if the superpowers like the US and Russia get involved. In World War, the world had witnessed the ugly face when such global and mighty forces got involved. It was now very important to finish the battle.

India again persuaded Pakistan to surrender if they didn't want to incur more losses. But General Niazi was ready to fight the war till the last Pakistani got martyred. So to teach Pakistan another lesson, the Indian Air Force bombed the Governor's house in Pakistan. This was the place where Pakistan used to plan for the war. This audacious move by India terrified Pakistan. On December 16, 1971, General Aurora gave thirty minutes of ultimatum to General Niazi to surrender. General Niazi immediately called for a unilateral ceasefire and surrendered its entire four-tier military to the Indian Army. Both Lt. Gen. Aurora and Gen. Niazi arrived at Dhaka racecourse where both Indian and Pakistani forces were present in large numbers. Lt. Gen. Niazi signed the instrument of surrender. He couldn't control his tears. 93,000 Pakistani soldiers surrendered to India. They took their guns and batches and placed them in front of the Indian Army. It was a very shameful situation

The Largest Surrender

for any army. This was one of the largest surrenders in modern history. India promised Pakistan to give away the conquered lands and keep the war prisoners safe and hand them over to Pakistan. They also wanted to tell the world that India was not an invader but helped weaker nations. This was the end of the Indo-Pak 1971 war and the birth of a new country—Bangladesh. Prime Minister Indira Gandhi also helped Sheikh Mujibur Rehman to set up the newly-formed country.

The after-effects of this war were very fruitful for India. International communities started taking India very seriously. They came to know that a South Asia superpower was in the making. India created a military and political dominance in Asia. This also gave confidence to India to conduct a nuclear test in 1974, three years after the war.

Women Against British

"Success isn't about the money you make, it is about the difference you make in people's lives."

– Michelle Obama

There is a certain section of people in India who are of the opinion that India became free from the British only because of the after-effects of World War II. The accepted notion is that the United Kingdom was bankrupt, and they had to sustain themselves, so, they left India and focused on their country. The reality was something different. Britain's economic position was relatively strong compared to its devastated European neighbours. In 1947, British exports to the world were equivalent in value to the combined exports of countries like France, Germany, Italy, Norway, Denmark, Belgium, the Netherlands, and Luxembo, who were also the fighters in the World War II.

Also, there is an opinion that there was nothing much left to loot from India. There is another opinion that because of British Raj, India got modernised and industrialised. These are some comments made by people who are unaware of our history and also lack empathy towards the incredible sacrifices of innumerable Indians.

Women Against British

Though the fight against the British was centralised or instructed by one political party, in numerous places, many people were fighting skirmishes by other ways apt for their way of thinking. In many such combats, these brave people failed, but the patriotism and their aim to breathe in free India was no less. From Kashmir to Kanyakumari and from Gujarat to northeast of India, the lust for freedom was there in the hearts of people everywhere. The British did try to implement a divide and rule policy but irrespective of caste, religion, creed, gender, everyone had only one purpose, and that was to attain freedom. So it was impossible for the British Raj to crush such big unrest among people.

Some of the freedom fighters were felicitated and received due respect after independence from the succeeding generations, but some just sank in oblivion. Every sacrifice, though, whether it was personal or material, was worth saluting and respecting.

One such woman was Bhogeswari Phukanani titled as the '60-year-old martyr', who sacrificed her life in serving Mother India. She was born in Nagaon, Assam, the northeastern part of India, in 1885. She was a simple homemaker and mother of eight children. It was a period when the Indian National Congress was fighting against the British on principles of nonviolence under the leadership of Mahatma Gandhi. He initiated the civil disobedience movement in the year 1930. This was a nationwide movement where many people took part voluntarily. The unrest towards the British government was created among the people to achieve independence by Lokmanya Bal Gangadhar Tilak. Under the guidance of Gandhiji, people were desperately working towards the attainment of freedom.

Bhogeswari was very active in the freedom struggle in the areas of Assam. She set up many offices of the Indian National Congress in Assam. Though she had some personal responsibilities, she took part in the civil disobedience movement and carried out a different protest against the British. She was arrested and jailed because of her participation in the freedom struggle. When she was in jail, the British seized some of the Indian National Congress offices near Assam and closed them. When she was released from jail, after some years of imprisonment, she gathered the like-minded people and re-opened the Congress office. Her grown-up children also helped her in this endeavour. It was a jubilant time for the nation lovers that they got their Indian National Congress office back from where they could again strike hard against British.

Along with her, many Assamese took part in the Quit India Movement. The environment of freedom struggle in Assam was taking its shape. The nation was singing the songs of freedom in one tone. The office's reopening was a big blow to the British Raj. They sent a large force to reclose the Congress office and to destroy it completely. This news reached Bhogeswari Devi. She, along with her sons and a large number of associates, went to safeguard the Congress office against the British police. The fashion of defence was nonviolent. Indians were waving the tricolour flag and singing *Vande Mataram* loudly. The

Women Against British

British, in their conventional way, acted against the side of humanity. The British had banned people from gathering and conducting politically motivated programmes. They were all set and ready with guns and *lathis* to stop people from protesting and to destroy the Congress office. The massive ambush took place between protestors and the British force. Many Indians were injured because of the violent attack from the force.

During the fight, one of the British officers grabbed India's national flag in the most disrespectful manner possible. Seeing this, Bhogeswari couldn't control her anger. She snatched the flag from the officer's hand and struck that officer with the pole of the flag and bruised him seriously. She was around 60 years of age when this incident happened. Still, the blow was so powerful that the British official got severely injured.

The British were using all their means to stop the protest. An officer named Finch understood that people won't stop the protest. Hence, he took out his gun and pointed it at the crowd. In that crowd, one of the sons of Bhogeswari was present. Bhogeswari noticed this. When he was about to shoot the people, Bhogeswari ran towards Finch and struck him with the pole so hard that he dropped his gun and fell on the ground. He somehow managed to get the gun and shoot Bhogeswari. She got seriously injured. She was taken to a hospital, but on the very next day, she succumbed to her injury. Her sacrifice for the country was no less important than any other freedom fighter. She had the choice of living a peaceful life with her family, but her love for the motherland motivated her to leave anything, everything and think only of the dearest *Bharatmata*. If we turn the pages of history, one can find many such examples of self-sacrifice for the country.

There was another selfless woman who spent every moment of her life in serving people. She lived for around 75 years, but since the age of ten, she had put all her life for the betterment of society. Her name is Rani Gaidinliu. She was born in the Tamenglong district of Manipur in northeast India. She was from the elite *Pamei* clan of the village. It was a tribal clan. She was a prodigious kid. Many traits of an amazing leader were displayed by her when she was merely eight years old. She had a great inclination towards spirituality at the age when kids would not be able to grasp regularities of life.

Her life took a turn when she met the goddesses daughter of Lord Bisnu (Lord Vishnu) in a forest. Lord Bisnu was a native God of *Zeliangrong* pantheon. Zeliangrong is a community consisting of people from Assam, Manipur, and Nagaland. She learnt many things from the goddesses. She also came to know about a man named Haipou Jadonang who later became her master and also the inspiration of her life. She developed a very close relationship with him and gained spiritual and political knowledge from him.

Haipou had started the *Heraka* movement in the year 1925 after witnessing the increase in forced Christianity in the northeastern region. Many missionaries of the West came to this land and tried to convert them to

Women Against British

Christianity by giving them false hope of a better life. Tribal people were easily deceived in such baits. The British were in full support of these conversions. They even provided required assistants to these missionaries. Many *Naga* (natives of Nagaland) people, the sons of the soil, got converted to Christianity under the influence of Christian missionaries. He wanted to stop this forceful conversion as the original religion of Naga was in danger.

Gaidinliu joined this moment when she was just fifteen years of age. Knowingly or unknowingly, she challenged the mighty British Raj as conversions were happening with the blessings of the British. Haipou, along with his followers, declared a war against the British to stop these conversions and the tortures Nagas were facing under the British. But before any formal war took place, he was arrested by the British army as they came to know that Haipou could be a danger to the British as he was gaining importance among people. They tortured him a lot in the prison to get information about anti-British activities happening in northeast India. But Haipou Jadonang was a hard nut to crack. He, with his strong willpower, did not serve their purpose. Hence, he was hanged in the jail by declaring him guilty in pseudo-murder charges.

This enraged Gaidinliu. She took out many protests against the British government for the heinous acts. The peace-loving and calm Rani had become a hardcore rebellion. Many fellow villagers opposed her violent means to fight against the government. But she, along with other disciples of Haipou Jadonang, were fuming inside. They wanted to bring down such an evil government and bring back the Naga dominance.

Rani Gaidinliu came to know about the civil disobedience movement. She asked the *Zeliangrong* group to join this movement. The rebellion in the northeast areas was very fierce under her leadership. Despite being a sixteen-year-old teenager, she was an effective orator, patriot and had great importance for the Zeliangrong people. The teenage girl became a reason for a headache for the British. She united everybody in northeastern India against the British. The government had announced a reward of Rs. 500/ – for the arrest of Rani.

Mr. J.P. Mills, the Deputy Commissioner of Naga Hills, was given the responsibility to crush Rani. He took the help of Assam rifles army and marched towards Bopungwami village in Naga Hills. They burnt down the whole village to ashes just to arrest Rani. But she managed to escape from there. A 16-year-old girl had become a major threat to British Raj in northeast India. She moved to Pulima village and started the work of building a fortress to fight against the British. She knew that her army needed to get ready for any kind of war-like situation. British Captain, Macdonald, made a surprise attack on Puilwa village early in the morning on October 17, 1932. Rani's army was completely surprised and could not offer any effective resistance. They surrendered, and Gaindiliu was arrested and then eventually jailed. She was sentenced to life imprisonment.

Women Against British

Pundit Jawaharlal Nehru tried a lot to get Rani released from jail, but all his attempts were futile. The British knew that if they release Rani, she will again bring people together and become a big nuisance for the government. Considering her influence over the people in the northeast government, she was not kept in the same jail for a long time. They shifted her to many prisons in Guwahati, Shillong, Aizawl, Tura, etc. Her followers continued the movement even after her arrest.

She was released from jail when India got independence in the year 1947. She had to spend her bright fifteen years of young womanhood in dark cells. She settled down at Tamenglong Headquarters and started a peaceful life. She met Prime Minister Jawaharlal Nehru and his daughter, Mrs. Indira Gandhi, in 1958.

She was appreciated by many great leaders across India. Atal Bihari Vajpayee, one of India's former Prime Ministers once said, "Any nation or country would be proud to have such a gifted woman who sacrificed everything for her people and for the cause she believed was good and true. She became a living legend in her lifetime."

She didn't stop after independence; rather, she continued her rebellion against the Naga National Council who were expanding their support for the increase of Christianity in Nagaland and adjoining areas.

Such was the significant contribution of many people in getting freedom for India. Today's freedom of speech, expression or choice didn't come to us as a gift or for free. There was a heavy loss of lives and property during the fight for freedom. We should not forget the contributions of the great freedom fighters. Because of them, we breathe free air. It is the responsibility of every citizen of the country to remember the sacrifices made for our well-being by such prodigious, noble people. We, Indians, should maintain sovereignty and work for our country so that our nation becomes stronger and better in every aspect of life.

Printed in Great
Britain
by Amazon